Cold Comfort

Cold Comfort

**One man's struggle to stop the illegal marketing
of powerful opioid drugs and save lives**

Bruce Boise

Foreword by Peter W. Chatfield, Partner, Phillips & Cohen LLP

BB Publishing, LLC | Dublin, OH

Published by
BB Publishing, LLC | Dublin, OH

Publisher's Cataloging-in-Publication Data
Boise, Bruce.

Cold comfort : one man's struggle to stop illegal marketing of powerful opioid drugs and save lives / Bruce Boise. – Dublin, OH : BB Pub., LLC, 2020.

p. ; cm.

ISBN13: 978-0-9601015-0-4

1. Cephalon, Inc.—Marketing. 2. Opioids—Labeling—Law and legislation—United States. 3. Drugs—Labeling—Law and legislation—United States. 4. Advertising—Drugs—Law and legislation—United States. I. Title.

KF3891.O3 B65 2020
344.7304233--dc23   2020905714

Project coordination by Jenkins Group, Inc.
www.BookPublishing.com

Interior layout by Brooke Camfield

Printed in the United States of America
24 23 22 21 20 • 5 4 3 2 1

DEDICATION

For my mother and father

Contents

Foreword

*F*or more than 25 years, it has been my great privilege as a lawyer to represent a rare subset of people who possess the courage and fortitude necessary to undertake the personal risks and costs of going to government authorities to stop fraudulent schemes that regularly cheat taxpayers and sometimes also put the public in danger.

Being a whistleblower is never easy. To gain the knowledge necessary to identify, prove, and weed out fraud, successful whistleblowers nearly always must first be insiders who become privy to details of high-stakes misconduct. For those unwilling to go along to get along in such situations, jobs and careers are routinely at stake. Personal safety can be as well.

Recognizing that fact, federal and state False Claims Acts—and other federal and state whistleblower reward programs—offer potentially lucrative rewards to those willing to undertake such risks. The rewards are given in order to compensate for the losses, suffering, hard work, and stress that virtually always come with being a whistleblower.

Defendants in whistleblower cases would have us believe that the whistleblower's own desire for wealth is the principal reason that allegations of fraud are made. In some cases that may be true.

In my experience, however, most people who become whistleblowers do so because their personal moral compass demands that they stop the wrongs they see. Indeed, some whistleblowers have no idea that any reward is possible when they first report wrongdoing. They blow the whistle because they must do so to be true to themselves.

Bruce Boise is that kind of whistleblower—and more. He blew the whistle after having experienced and enjoyed great success as a pharmaceutical sales representative and manager while Cephalon Inc., the company he worked for, was growing in a rapid and still-lawful way. He blew the whistle because Cephalon became addicted to ever-increasing sales profits it could not maintain lawfully through on-label sales of the pharmaceutical drugs it owned. He could not continue to stray with them. He blew the whistle on Cephalon because he knew patients' health and lives were at stake.

Unaware at the time that any reward was even possible, he risked—and lost—everything by alerting the FDA to Cephalon's fraud and by wearing a wire to help prove his allegations. He suffered as much as any whistleblower I have ever known. Yet he rarely complained and, even then, always apologetically.

By the time he learned a reward was possible and was thereafter able to find legal help to bring suit, Bruce went from first in line to expose the fraud to third in line for a reward by filing a qui tam lawsuit. He thus lost most of what he could have received if he had found a lawyer and filed his False Claims Act case first, before jumping in to help the FDA simply do what he felt was right.

Bruce Boise is the very best kind of whistleblower. I am proud that I had the opportunity to help him navigate the experience, prove his case, and rebuild his and his family's financial foundation for moving forward with his life. It was an honor to fight by his side.

Peter W. Chatfield, Partner, Phillips & Cohen LLP
www.phillipsandcohen.com

Acknowledgments

*O*nce upon a time, Peter Chatfield said I should do a book that could help others who dared to embark on the difficult road to whistleblowing, and so I did. Thank you for that encouragement, your brilliant legal mind, and continued mentorship.

Thank you, Tim Harper, my ghostwriter, who captured my story, in every detail.

I will never forget the support and love of my three children: Eric, Michelle, and Meredith, along with that of my best friend and brother, Rex.

Author's Note

*T*his is my story, told from my perspective, giving my personal narrative behind the headlines. I am not trying to show what it is like for everyone to be a federal informant or whistleblower. I am not claiming credit for foreseeing the opioid epidemic. But my story, what happened to me, and what I made happen may be valuable for individuals and organizations dealing with corruption, fraud, corporate malfeasance, or other wrongdoing. My story, I hope, will also point out how a perfect storm can grow out of an innovative pharmaceutical company, its aggressive leadership, its enthusiastic employees, and its well-meaning customers—the doctors who followed bad advice and wrote prescriptions that put some of their patients at unnecessary risk.

Everything in this book is true, based on my notes, electronic recordings, government records, private reference sources, and the best of my memory. The names have been changed for several people to obscure their identities; they are private people, not public figures. They can raise their hands and speak up if they want to be identified. Some have, already, in outing themselves to journalists reporting on my story and my book. If a person in the book is identified only by a single first name, that is a pseudonym for a private person. People identified by their full names are public figures who operate in a world with different expectations of privacy.

One of those public figures is Peter Chatfield, the lawyer who handled my case and helped me get through the long, arduous, and often painful years of frustration, fear, self-doubt, and despair while the case was dragging and I was struggling in so many ways. I owe Peter a huge debt of thanks.

Personally, I need to thank all the people in Key West who supported me and embraced me through thick and thin. There are too many close friends to mention here by name, but you all know who you are.

I can never do enough to thank my family for their support and encouragement, even when things were the darkest. They suffered, too. But my brother, Rex, my late mother, my ex-wife, Beth, and especially my three kids—Eric, Michelle, and Meredith—never complained, even when they had every right to. Instead, they were totally supportive and encouraging, telling me I was doing the right thing. The kids' support brought us closer together as a family and made me a stronger person. I'll be forever grateful to them.

Bruce Boise
Dublin, Ohio
May 2020

One

We Were the Good Guys

*M*y colleagues and I, and the company we worked for, were supposed to be part of the healing. We were supposed to be the good guys, helping people. The helpers. If we made some money along the way, well, that's fine. That was fair. We should be paid, and sometimes paid well, for doing a good job and helping a lot of people. If we helped doctors prescribe the most effective drugs, we were helping many more patients lead happier, healthier, more productive lives. It was easy to believe in what we were doing as doing good, almost a noble cause. I probably could have ended up as a good salesman selling almost anything. I could have sold complicated medical instruments from one big institution to another. I could have traded stocks or bonds or commodities. I could have sold industrial carpeting to skyscrapers. I could have

1

helped shuttered Rust Belt factories and closed-up shopping malls be taken over by other enterprises that would adapt them to the twenty-first century, like Amazon or marijuana farms.

But I liked selling pharmaceuticals—not selling them directly to patients but by informing doctors who knew more than I did about medicine and healing and prescribing and human conditions. By providing the medical community with up-to-date information, free samples, and good clinical information, I was helping doctors help their patients. It was a good feeling for me. Society had a lot of problems, and I was playing a small role as a solution to one of the biggest problems—health care. It didn't hurt that there were compensations. Sure, the money was great. I was doing really well. I won a lot of awards from both companies I worked for when they recognized my abilities as a sales rep.

Beyond the money and the recognition, though, was the fun. I got a real kick out of working with doctors, studying medical journals, doing everything I could to be part of the overall team that was helping patients. I liked the other people I worked with, too, mostly other guys in the early days, but with more and more women, including in sales and management roles, as the years went on. It felt like I was part of a convivial, collegial team—not just at my company but also in the pharmaceutical sales field in general. We were smart. We were ambitious. Sure, we had good-natured competition within our company and with other companies. But in the end, everyone saw the big picture: to help people. It was a great career for me.

Well, that's the way it was for almost 20 years—until it wasn't.

It turns out we were not just peddling drugs that could hurt a few people if misprescribed. No, it turned out that part of what my colleagues and I were doing back then, back in the late 1990s and early 2000s, was unknowingly, unwittingly, sowing the seeds of what became perhaps America's biggest health challenge of the era: the opioid epidemic. Some of those feel-good painkillers weren't just making people feel good and weren't just killing pain. They were killing people. Looking back, I wonder whether there are things that could have been done—by me but especially by the authorities—back then to cut the head off the opioid snake just as it was slithering its way into American society and before it caused hundreds of thousands of overdose deaths.

Two

What Is "Off-Label"?

*A*nyone who has ever picked up a prescription has seen the exhaustive labeling, even on simple, straightforward drugs. Here's what it is, what it's for, how often to take it, and, in the fine print, the usual long list of warnings and side effects. The bottom line: drugs are supposed to be prescribed only for what is "on label." What they were "indicated for," in pharma-talk. If a certain treatment was approved on the label, the drug was "indicated" for that treatment.

Sometimes, though, a drug can be effective in treating ailments or conditions that it isn't indicated for. Prescribing drugs for treatments that the FDA has not approved them for is considered "off-label."

Off-label prescribing by doctors is not illegal, or even unusual, in the history of the pharmaceutical industry and the practice of medicine. Doctors are allowed to prescribe off-label for their patients if they think it might help them.

A drug company sales rep's job is to promote the company's drugs and tell doctors who the drugs could help and how—but only within the government-approved guidelines for that drug. The government-approved guidelines for any drug are found printed on the "package insert" for that drug. The PI, as it's known in the pharmaceutical industry, has all the scientific facts of any drug (pharmacology, pharmacodynamics, controlled studies, dosing, contraindications, and more). It is illegal for drug reps to suggest to doctors that they prescribe any drug off-label for a treatment not approved by the federal Food and Drug Administration from the PI.

The reason for this is simple: the doctor and the drug rep have different jobs. One is to treat the patient and the other is to sell the drug's benefits from the PI.

We were sales representatives, not gangsters, though. Our role was to do good. We traveled to our assigned sales areas or territories, met with doctors, and told them about the benefits of the various drugs that our company made and sold. We made small talk with the doctors about their families. We asked about their business and talked with them about their patients, what prescriptions they were writing, and what was working and not working.

We asked what sorts of medical problems their patients were struggling with and tried to give doctors information that would provide new strategies for helping those patients. We made suggestions for new or modified treatment and left the doctors with free samples they could pass along to their patients. If a patient tried a new drug from one of our samples and it worked—if it helped—the doctor would prescribe it. The sale would be recorded through the pharmacy that filled the prescription and reported back to the pharmaceutical company.

If a doctor prescribed one of the company's drugs, the sales rep serving that doctor got credit for the sale and got a commission from the company based on the sales for that month. When the pharmaceutical sales system worked, it worked well, and it helped everybody. Sales reps like me got their commissions, the doctors helped their patients, and—best of all—the patients themselves were healthier. They could lead better, fuller lives and have a higher quality of life. I loved being a pharmaceutical sales rep, and I was pretty good at it.

In the early 2000s, Cephalon began encouraging doctors to prescribe some of our drugs, especially the ones not selling particularly well, for some unintended, untested, unproven treatment. Sometimes the drugs worked for these unintended purposes; sometimes they didn't. When off-label prescription drugs worked for new and different treatments, doctors looked like geniuses for coming up with this creative new way of using an old drug. The drug company got more sales, and the sales reps got more commissions. On the other hand, sometimes an off-label prescription backfired. It made the patient worse.

Off-label marketing is unethical and illegal and potentially dangerous for patients. My company seemed to be ignoring both the potential dangers to patients and legal issues. This was the second drug company I had worked for as a sales rep and manager, and there had been ethical, potential legal problems at my first employer, too. Those issues drove me away from my first company to take a better job at what I thought was a better company. But here I was, in my second company, facing another ethical dilemma.

The sales reps who worked for me—I had become an area manager—were not simply being asked to sell our drugs off-label. We were being encouraged and trained—and paid very well—to sell our drugs off-label, for medical conditions those drugs had never been expected to treat and were not designed to treat. The threats to our jobs if we didn't cooperate were becoming less subtle. To work for this company, you needed to show off-label sales results.

I complained, first to my closest coworkers, then to my bosses. I didn't think selling off-label was right or could ever be justified. It was wrong and not solely because of the federal regulations specifically prohibiting off-label marketing. It was dangerous to unsuspecting patients. I was afraid someone was going to die.

I was starting to be seen as a problem within the company—the one guy who was trying to rain on everybody's parade, who was trying to squelch all these off-label sales that were helping our reps earn big salaries, often hundreds of thousands of dollars. I complained, but my complaints fell on deaf ears.

Most sales reps didn't seem to care or shrugged it off. After all, it was the doctors doing the prescribing, not us sales reps. We were just providing information. If something bad happened, it wasn't our fault. And, hey, did you see the sales numbers for last month? We were getting rich from selling drugs off-label, whether they worked or not. It didn't take long for the hypocrisy to get to me. My career suffered. My sales suffered. In turn, my relationships suffered, not just at work. I took my unhappiness home with me and paid the price for it eventually.

When I stumbled into whistleblowing, it was more by accident than on purpose. I didn't go looking for the authorities. Someone else saw what was happening and confronted me and challenged me to step up. I had no idea what it would cost me. If I had known then what I know now, things might have been different. If I had known what my life would be like as a whistleblower—the rest of my life, actually—I might have thought more carefully about that first meeting with two federal agents in a nondescript franchise hotel lobby.

Greg wasn't an FBI agent, but he was with a comparable, parallel investigative arm within the federal Food and Drug Administration, the FDA's Office of Criminal Investigations. The role of his agency was to investigative wrongdoing within the pharmaceutical industry. Sometimes the drug companies paid fines—often very large fines, in the tens or hundreds of millions of dollars. In especially egregious cases, the investigations led the

Department of Justice to seek prison time for the people involved; they could be management and all the way up to the CEO.

In 2019, the opioid maker Insys was fined $225 million for off-label marketing of its sublingual fentanyl spray, SUBSYS, a powerful but highly addictive opioid painkiller. In this case, reps, managers, and executives were arrested for racketeering.

Nearly 20 years earlier, Cephalon's drug Actiq, a potent opioid, a hundred times stronger than morphine and administered by a lollipop, was one of the handfuls of drugs that the company was peddling in off-label promotion that year.

"Bruce," asked the agent, "will you wear a wire?"

Three

My Career Path to Selling Pharmaceuticals

I grew up in the small town of Troy, Ohio, in the 1950s and '60s. My dad was a dentist, my mom a housewife. They had two sons: me and my twin, Rex, 10 minutes younger. It was a household with a lot of discipline—not harsh discipline, not punishment, not abuse. I'm talking about discipline in terms of doing the right thing, living the right way, working hard, being kind and considerate to others, and respecting rules and authority, starting with your parents.

My dad was a World War II veteran and a medic in the all-Ohio 37th Division that was the tip of the spear for the central battles in the Pacific Theatre. He entered the army as a private in the National Guard and was battlefield commissioned a first lieutenant. In the four years that he served in the Pacific, he'd seen a lot and done a lot—maybe too much—on the battlefield, especially in the brutal battle against the Japanese to take Guadalcanal.

It was the first full-on assault by American forces on Japanese territory, and the Japanese fought bitterly, to the death. My dad distinguished himself amid that fierce fighting and elsewhere. He was awarded a Bronze Star and a Silver Star, the third-highest medal of valor for US troops. I have a photo of General Beightler personally pinning a medal on him. But the war wasn't all parades and medals for my dad. He was almost court-martialed once when he was supervising a company of soldiers who were all African Americans.

Their barracks were shabbily built on a swampy area, and the construction of the floor was so bad that the soldiers were getting sick from the stinking, bug-infested mud coming up through the floor of their barracks. So my dad ripped some of the excess decorative siding off the much fancier barracks that housed American officers—their own floorboards were nice and tight, no bugs, no mud—and he installed that siding as a new floor in the African American barracks. Everybody then, both black and white soldiers, had a nice, dry floor. My dad was threatened with charges and time in the stockade for tearing apart the officers' housing: "damage to government property."

I'm not sure how he avoided the court-martial. I suspect it would have been more trouble than it was worth for his commanding officers, especially if there was a prospect of the African American soldiers supporting him or a reporter from

Stars and Stripes covering the trial. Besides that, my dad was a good officer and a good medic, and he was needed on the front lines. If it had happened during peacetime, when he wasn't needed to lead men into battle, he probably would have been court-martialed.

My dad grew up poor, but he was very intelligent and a very caring person. His dream was always to be a doctor—until he went to war and saw more blood and gore than anyone should face in a lifetime. He wanted to forget about the war when he came home. He had seen enough death and didn't want to face more death in his daily work. But he still wanted to help and serve people, so he became a dentist. He was a fastidious man, in every way. He shaved every day and always wore a white shirt, even on weekends. One of my most vivid memories came from a weekend when my brother and I, very young, were in the car with my dad and we came upon a horrific traffic accident with multiple serious injuries. Some cars were driving past, slowing down only to gawk before heading down the highway again at full speed. We stopped. "Stay in the car, boys," he ordered.

We watched, pressed up against the car windows, as our dad moved from person to person, doing triage, applying a tourniquet here and over there shifting someone's position to reduce shock and slow the flow of blood. Over one person he stopped only briefly; he examined the person's wounds, gently eased the victim into a more comfortable position, said a few words, and then moved on. That person, my brother and I could sense, was going to die soon. Our dad couldn't do anything for him, so he moved on to see whether he could help the next victim. When he finally came back to the car, his white shirt was soaked in blood. That's what I mean when I talk about discipline and duty and responsibility in our household. He was the town dentist and handled a lot of the ER calls late at night.

In some ways, my brother and I never fit in with the other kids in our small town. We were both big guys, strong and athletic. But my dad never let us play sports. Too frivolous, he believed. I remember the high school coach coming to our house to talk to my dad when I was 13 and already well over six feet tall, the summer before I started eighth grade. The coach had heard I was a good pickup basketball player and had come by a playground to watch me play. After he saw me dunking the ball and dominating the game against high school guys, he drove over to our house to talk to my dad.

"I know he's only in eighth grade," the coach said, "but kids that young are allowed to play on the high school team in their school district, and he could really help our team this season. He could play varsity basketball for five seasons and maybe get a college scholarship, maybe a full ride, maybe even to Ohio State." Ohio State was the dream for most kids growing up in Ohio in those days—certainly, it was for me.

"No," my dad said. No explanation. Just no. The coach tried to appeal, and my dad politely escorted him out of the house. I never did play high school basketball or any other sports, though the coach would sometimes have his players scrimmage—play a practice game—against pickup teams Rex and I would pull together just for the heck of it. We won our fair share of those games against the varsity team. The coach was furious at his team whenever that happened. The pickup teams Rex and I pulled together were usually the two of us and some of our friends from the recreation center in Troy's small black community. That's where we hung out most of the time, for basketball and for other stuff like dancing. On community rec nights, the gym would be open for a couple of hours for pickup basketball, and then the school janitor would turn down the lights a little and someone would spin 45 records and people would dance. Rex and I learned to play hoops and dance with the black kids—everybody liked the Temptations, for their dance moves—and both of those skills served us well in life, especially the dancing.

Another reason we didn't fit in with the other kids in our small town is that we didn't spend summers in Troy. My dad acquired a small lot on a small lake an hour away when we were kids, and we spent our summers there. My dad had put himself through dental school on crews working construction in the post-WWII home-building boom, so he decided he would build our lake house himself—with Rex and I providing the grunt labor. I remember taking 75-pound bags of roof shingles up a ladder. I was allergic to bees, and once I got attacked on the roof by hornets and came scrambling down the ladder. "Dammit," my dad said, "they're not bullets. Get back to work." He was a wonderful guy, my dad, but looking back, I can see how he never really escaped that war experience. I wonder what his life would have been like—and my childhood—if he hadn't gone through so much.

Despite all the construction work, summers at the lake were fun. There were a few other kids Rex and I hung out with, and we kept busy swimming, fishing, sailing our little boat, water skiing, and occasionally sneaking out on warm evenings to drink a little beer. My brother and I were good kids, and so were the other kids we hung out with at the lake. But because we had this other life at the lake, we missed out on a lot of the growing-up-in-a-neighborhood stuff back in Troy. While the other kids our age were bonding over the summertime, we were away. We came back every autumn like we were new kids just moving to town.

Rex loved to tease people, whether they deserved it or not. He wasn't a malicious guy, but he gave people grief and zeroed in on their weaknesses. I think he was just trying to get a rise out of them and spark some sort of interaction that could lead them to become friends. Instead, he most often sparked some sort of interaction that led to hard feelings. I got to be pretty good at stepping in between Rex and other people and once in a while pulling people off of Rex.

When Rex and I finally got to Ohio State, we mostly paid our own way from our after-school jobs, with some help from our folks and some student loans, though nothing like what kids today have to take on. We roomed together. Finally out of the house, I decided to participate in organized sports. I walked on to try out for the Buckeyes basketball team. It went about as well as expected, but I got cut after a couple of weeks of tryouts. I was as physically talented as a lot of the players who were there on scholarship, but I had little idea of the basics of the game.

Maybe the coaches thought it would have taken too much effort to try to teach me the stuff the other guys had been learning from coaches since third grade. I was OK with that. I knew I could play college basketball if I really devoted a year to private coaching and learning all the fundamentals and catching up, but that would have been pretty much a full-time job and wasn't what I had in mind at age 18.

I wanted to just be a typical college student, and I loved the whole Ohio State experience—being away from home, going to classes, meeting lots of new people. The only thing bothering me was my grades. I was not a good student. Never had been. At Ohio State, I thought I might want to follow in the footsteps of an uncle who was a retired Air Force lieutenant colonel and had worked in the early NASA program. I wanted to be like him: a rocket scientist. My family, to put it mildly, did not think I was rocket scientist material. I had trouble absorbing what I read and processing it. My folks never said anything explicitly, but I am pretty confident that they thought Rex was the smart one and I was the nice one. Nice but dumb. When I realized in college that I wasn't up to the math and physics needed for rocket science, I set my sights on law. I would be a lawyer. That dream didn't last long, either. Too much reading. Too much analysis. At the end of my sophomore year, I was running out of dreams.

Desperate, I went back to school for the autumn of my junior year with a new resolve. I was going to simply keep reading and rereading everything for my courses and memorizing as much of it as I could. Suddenly, I was getting not my usual Bs and Cs but As.

I realized I was not a dumb guy. I was a smart guy who had been studying the wrong way. It wasn't until I was in my thirties that I was diagnosed as dyslexic—nobody knew the term back in the 1960s—and realized that was why I had so much trouble with the written word. I also realized, as time went on and I became a better student and a better learner, that I had always been held back by not being a linear thinker. Logic didn't work for me the way it did for most people: this means that, and that means something else. Instead of thinking in a linear way, A to B to C, I naturally think more peripherally. I absorb everything, including the random and the seemingly inapplicable, and put it all together: this means that, but something else no one thought of might make this and that something entirely new and different.

It was liberating for me to learn this about myself and to start to use my way of peripheral thinking to build new relationships between ideas and with people. That peripheral way of thinking almost ruined my academic career during my first two years at Ohio State, but it turned out to be invaluable later in my college career and throughout life.

After trying chemistry and engineering and political science and even physical education at Ohio State, I finally graduated in 1972 with majors in political science and history and a minor in geology. I could have moved back home with my folks. Rex did, and that helped him afford to continue his education to become an architect. I got along well with my folks for the rest of their lives—my dad died in 1997 and my mom in 2012—but it didn't feel right to me to go back home. I wanted to be on my own, and I think they were fine with that. I had a quick one-year starter marriage and a brief stab at grad school in geology at the University of Akron. Then I knocked around for a few years between Akron and Columbus. I sold jewelry. I managed a sporting goods store. I married Beth, and we started a family.

Up to that point, in the late 1970s, in my late twenties, the job at the sporting goods store was the best I had ever had. I was making a grand sum of $9,000 a year, and Beth and I were crazy in love and raising three little kids. But I knew that kind of job was not the sort of life I wanted. I didn't like going to work on a schedule someone posted for me every week, including weekends, too, because so many people shop for sporting goods on Saturdays. It grated on me, bringing home that same paycheck no matter how well I did at work and just hoping for a raise of a few percentage points every year. I talked to Beth about it, and she sympathized. But she didn't want me to do anything rash. She liked that I had a steady job. We could make it work, she said, and maybe I could go back to grad school someday. But not just yet, while we had these little kids to feed. Still, there had to be something more in life for me than managing a sporting goods store.

I had a lot of hassles with my boss. He often wanted me to do something the way he wanted it done, rather than the more efficient and productive way I wanted it done. This boss liked ultimatums, and he used them a lot on employees. He knew we needed our jobs, especially me, the store manager with the little kids at home. It all came to a head one morning when he called me and told me to come in early and work for him—to do a double shift at the store that day—because he was hungover and needed to go back to bed.

I'd had enough. "No," I said. "Mail my last check to me." I started applying for jobs that same day, combing through the local newspapers, which back then had pages and pages of help wanted ads.

One of the first ads I answered was for a job as a sales rep with a pharmaceutical company. I knew a little about what that job entailed, but it seemed at first like an odd choice because growing up, I knew that my dad didn't like sales reps. He often welcomed them into his dental practice when they wanted to come in and talk about their latest products. "I do that so I can throw them out," he told me. I had seen it many times. When I was looking at the help wanted ads posted by drug companies, I thought, Hey, my dad is really tough on pharmaceutical reps. I know what it must be like to deal with a doc who is reluctant to sit down with a sales rep. I'll probably never encounter a doctor who is tougher than my dad.

And I never did.

Four

The Sales Rep—A Part
of the Health-Care Team

*W*hat little I knew about pharmaceutical sales representative jobs sounded interesting. It wasn't retail, like working in a sporting goods store. Sales representatives had bosses, but the reps spent a lot of their time on the road, visiting doctors and hospitals, telling them about the company's products, and then filling out order forms. The job seemed to offer the sort of independence that would suit me, along with an ever-changing list of tasks. Every day I'd visit different people and have different conversations. I hated the idea of working all day at a desk, no matter what the job. Too boring.

I interviewed for three pharmaceutical sales jobs and accepted one of them, with Carter-Wallace. Carter-Wallace was a relatively small and undistinguished pharmaceutical firm with a history dating back to the nineteenth century. It was not regarded as a "high-science" company, the term often used to describe pharmaceutical firms large and small that spent a lot on research and development and led the way in bringing the world innovative new drugs and new treatments. Back then, in the early 1980s, Carter-Wallace was focused more on everyday, uncomplicated treatments, along with mundane personal care products such as deodorants, condoms, and laxatives. The company also sold a small range of handheld medical devices and manufactured a few drugs itself. It was a small range of prescription drugs, such as tranquilizers and muscle relaxants, which Carter-Wallace marketed to doctors and hospitals—and that's where the sales reps came in, including me.

A rep received a modest monthly salary, with most of the annual income coming from commissions and bonuses based on that rep's sales totals. If the whole sales team or the whole company exceeded its goals, everybody might get a bonus at the end of the year. From scratching out a living at around $9,000 a year as the assistant manager of a sporting goods store, selling basketballs and baseball bats and jockstraps, I was soon making $50,000 a year. I didn't know anyone else my age who was making that much money or anywhere close to it. Curious, I looked it up the other day, and that $50,000 back then has the purchasing power of about $150,000 today—still pretty good money today for anybody in their late twenties. Beth and I had three little kids, but we still had plenty of discretionary income, and we used it to feather our nest, indulge ourselves and our kids, and generally enjoy life. I was one of the up-and-comers at Carter-Wallace, with a bright future in pharmaceutical sales. We loved our lives in Dublin, Ohio, with a nice house and nice cars and nice vacations and good kids. We had it all, and things were just getting better.

Carter-Wallace, like most pharma companies, had an extensive training program for its sales reps, especially new, young people like me, with no experience. The company and its trainers wanted to educate us about drugs in general and the company's products in particular, but that wasn't the main focus of the training. The training was designed, above all, to teach us to *sell*. During that training, I came to see why there's an old saying: "A good salesman can sell anything." Another old saying is something like, "A real salesman's best product is himself." I came to see that, yes, no matter what drug products I was selling, I was selling myself, too. If my customers liked me and trusted me, I would sell more—and earn more in commissions.

I owe a lot to the managers and trainers at Carter-Wallace who helped me learn the ropes, especially a dapper guy named Trevor, my trainer in the early part of my career, the guy who broke me into the pharmaceutical business—and into sales. Trevor was a natural leader, tall and well spoken. He commanded a room. He was a central figure in a major change that was going on in the pharmaceutical industry in the 1980s when drug company sales reps began to serve doctors as unofficial consultants. Instead of telling doctors, "Here are my products; please buy them," drug sales reps were trained to tell doctors, "What kinds of problems are you seeing in your practice? Maybe some of my products can help them. Let's talk about it." I vividly remember Trevor, a master in the consulting process and a master negotiator, confronting me early in my training. "What's up with you?" he demanded. "You move around like you're embarrassed by your own presence." I was offended, but I also genuinely wanted to know what he was talking about.

"You're a big guy," he said. "That's you, who you are. But you move like a little guy. It's almost like you're meek. You don't want to call attention to yourself. You're a big guy. Embrace that. Make it work for you." Trevor told me I needed to change the way I saw myself—and the way others saw me, from the first time they met me and every time they met me—starting with my size, six foot three, well north of 200 pounds. "When you walk into a room, own it," Trevor instructed me. "You're the biggest guy in the room, the biggest presence. People notice you and want to find out who you are, what you know, what is this big guy like?"

Trevor helped me see how much natural ability I had. Embracing my physical presence was a big part of that. I might have been a better salesman because I often didn't feel like I fit in while growing up; that outsider experience helped me sense other people's discomfort and how they sometimes didn't feel like they were fitting in. I also had a kind of intuition that was a by-product of my peripheral thinking. I was able to latch onto seemingly unrelated facts and then see how they fit together— and how they worked for me. For whatever reason, I found that I could tap into an ability to read people and get them to talk about their concerns and motivations. It all started with listening and being interested in other people's stories. That empathy helped me become a good sales rep. I was the rep who got doctors to talk about what was bothering them in their practice, their toughest cases, their fears for their most troubled patients, and their hopes for helping those patients. When I met doctors, I found that if we talked a bit—mostly the doctors talking, me listening—we might have a conversation leading to my suggestions that might help the doctors figure out what they really wanted and how it could be accomplished. More often than not, what doctors really wanted from pharmaceutical company sales reps was assistance in identifying the drugs that would help patients the most, especially patients with difficult medical conditions. They made choices that they decided were best for their patients and best for them. And best for me.

For a time, I thought I wanted to be a trainer, like Trevor, who had helped me so much. I wanted to help other people the way Trevor had helped me. It felt like he had unlocked a magic kingdom for me, and I wanted to do that for others. But I was the only one who thought that was a good idea. Everybody else in the company discouraged me, including Trevor. He said what everybody else said: "Bruce, you're crazy to want to be a trainer. You're too good a salesman to be hidden away as a trainer. You need to be out there selling. It's best for the company, for the doctors, for the patients, and for you and your family." It was true: I'd make less money as a trainer.

But at the same time, I noted, Trevor had chosen the trainer path. He hadn't become a top sales rep even though he obviously knew how to sell. Why had he stayed a trainer? Trevor grimaced when I asked him that. "Bruce," he said, "I would have loved to be a sales representative. I would love to be out there, fighting the fight, in the trenches, doing it every day like you guys do. But I just wasn't very good at it. I tried being a sales rep for a while, and let's just say I'm a better sales trainer than a sales rep." Trevor later was able to use his strong leadership skills to become a successful sales manager even though he himself rarely went out on sales calls the way his sales reps did. He wasn't selling, but he was managing the people who were selling, and he was a hell of a coach. He found a way to succeed by recognizing and compensating for his shortcomings, by trying new things and using what he was good at. In the end, maybe that was Trevor's biggest and best lesson for me: be open-minded, set high goals, try everything, push the boundaries—and in the end, know yourself, what you can do, and what you should be doing. One of the most important things I learned from Trevor was to identify my own personal strengths and to play to those strengths. Trevor advised me to know when it's time to stay in my lane and concentrate my best years on doing what I do best. For years, I tried to do that. Most of the time. But those other times—straying out of my lane—are what this story is about.

At Carter-Wallace, I quickly learned and became absorbed into the working patterns and habits of "detail men," as pharmaceutical reps were typically called back in the day. Nearly all were men back in the 1980s, but even the women were called "detail men," too, until the ranks of women in the sales jobs grew and the antiquated term was dropped in favor of the all-inclusive "sales rep."

The way it usually worked was each rep had a specific territory, and each rep had one or more specific products to sell. One rep wouldn't stray into another rep's territory, and one rep wouldn't sell another rep's products. Reps would roam their territories, usually via a new car provided by the company or, nowadays, an SUV. Free gas, free insurance, free maintenance—great side benefits. We'd do our rounds, visiting doctors' offices, clinics, and hospitals and sitting down with physicians and talking.

Here's how the prescription medicine industry works. Pharmaceutical companies produce drugs and sell them to wholesalers. Wholesalers sell the drugs to retail pharmacies, which then pass the medicine along to patients based on prescriptions written for the patients by their doctors. Drug companies assign their sales reps to specific physicians. The reps call on those physicians regularly. When one of those doctors on a sales rep's roster writes a prescription and the patient fills it, paying with cash or insurance or both at a retail pharmacy, the sale is recorded by the pharmacy and passed along to the drug company. If a doctor writes a prescription and a patient gets it filled, the company's sales rep gets credit for the sale. Pharmaceutical companies pay their sales reps largely on a commission basis, according to how many prescriptions are written by the doctor for the company's various medicines—the drugs put in front of that particular doctor by that company's sales rep.

More prescriptions mean more revenue for the drug company and more profits, as well as more commissions and higher earnings for the company's sales reps.

I was assigned a group of doctors to call on for Carter-Wallace. My goal as a sales rep was to persuade, convince—sell—those doctors on Carter-Wallace's stable of prescription drugs. As a newly minted drug sales representative, I might be assigned to call on Dr. Smith. I'd talk to Dr. Smith about Carter-Wallace's drugs—always in a very positive light—and hope that Dr. Smith would write prescriptions for his or her patients for those drugs. The more of those prescriptions that were written by Dr. Smith and filled by Dr. Smith's patients, the more I earned in commissions. Beyond the sheer sales numbers, along the way, I tried to build a relationship, a rapport, with Dr. Smith. It was a relationship business. That's the way it worked at Carter-Wallace and pretty much every other drug company.

I soon grew comfortable calling on doctors, asking questions, and providing information based on what doctors told me. What drugs did they need to be restocked? How were the drugs we supplied performing in the practice or at the clinic or in the hospital? Were the drugs helping patients? Were the doctors satisfied? Had the doctors considered this other drug we sell? Excuse me, doctor, did we tell you that our prescription drug is actually better than that other drug from the other competing pharmaceutical company? Have you seen the latest study results? I learned that the bible for every drug is the PI, the package insert. These are the instructions, including recommended uses and possible side effects, that come with every pharmaceutical product. You've seen them every time you pick up a prescription from the drug store and open the box, and you've probably thrown away lots of them without reading a word. We drug reps memorized those inserts and knew them chapter and verse so we could talk knowledgeably with doctors.

One of the sales rep's most powerful incentives was and is the free sample: giving doctors' offices copious supplies of free drugs to persuade the doctors to hand out to patients—and then to write prescriptions for those drugs. Ideally—and it happened remarkably often—a doctor would try a new drug simply because a drug rep had handed out some free samples. Doctors loved free samples, mostly because their patients did. Who doesn't like free samples? Many people have learned that when their doctor writes a new prescription, the standard question from the patient is, "Do you have any free samples of that, doctor?" Samples always went fast, especially for more costly or hard-to-get drugs.

It's easy to see how the relationship between an individual doctor can develop with a particular sales rep who is prompt and helpful with products and information. Good sales reps help doctors do their jobs. They save doctors time and effort and offer doctors insights that they might not have. A doctor might have to read several medical journals a week to learn what a drug company rep can pass along with a five-minute visit. Some doctors want as little to do with drug companies as they can manage—like my dad—but many others are at least cordial and sometimes friendly.

I quickly learned that most doctors were happy to have a sales rep's perspective. After all, we were the experts on our drugs. Sure, drug reps could provide useful information and free samples, sometimes even helpful updates on their products. When asked about other drugs for the same medical condition, a rep could know the competition in the market and relay features and benefits.

Sometimes a business relationship develops: the drug sales rep will arrange for the doctor to get a free trip or a cruise or an appearance honorarium in exchange for talking about—and talking up—what medicine the drug company is promoting the most at that moment. Some critics might say that is a conflict of interest for a drug company to pay a doctor in exchange for prescribing the drug company's products. But it is the way things have been done in the pharmaceutical industry forever as a way of plugging into continuing medical education (CME).

Doctors are required to attend and get credit for a certain number of classes, talks, and discussions every year in order to keep their licenses. Medical knowledge is always changing and always advancing, and CME requirements are designed to make sure doctors keep abreast of new developments. They also happened to be a place where drugs, off-label, could be discussed and validated by physicians.

Five

They Trusted Me

I was soon promoted to Carter-Wallace's CNS division, handling drugs for the central nervous system. I was assigned to call on doctors and market drugs in the field of neurology, the science and treatment of the central nervous system and brain. I loved the work. I grew close to a group of young neurologists at a hospital in Cincinnati. I threw myself into neurology, while reading the journals, showing up at lectures, and going with the Department of Neurology doctors to grand rounds. I sat in on patient interviews and examinations and consultations—always with prior approval, of course. The doctors began calling me "EKG Boise" for the way I would read and interpret the jagged-line results of electrocardiogram printouts. The young doctors, mostly residents, treated me like I was a resident, too—one of them. "Hey, Bruce, what does this line on the test mean?" they'd ask.

I'd usually know or make a good guess. If I was wrong, they'd patiently explain why. Sometimes I offered our products as a possible solution for a patient who wasn't responding to the usual medication or therapy. They would talk about the patients and whether surgery was appropriate at that point, and they'd be explaining what they needed to do and the risks and possible outcomes, and I'd be soaking it all up. Sometimes they let me shadow them in clinics. I'd be in a white coat like the doctors were wearing, but I would be in the background. I never said anything, but I watched and listened intently—and learned a lot.

Afterward, when we weren't around patients, I was encouraged to ask lots of questions, and I did. I became close to one young doctor in particular. He was a really smart, personable guy in his mid thirties, a few years younger than me, and seemed really interested in fostering my knowledge of neurology and my understanding of how doctors serve their patients. We became friendly. I admired him greatly, and I knew he respected me, too, because he gave me so many opportunities to see and learn at the hospital. He trusted me. And that trust meant a great deal to me. It seemed like I was a small, unofficial part of the team, and that felt great.

This was a teaching hospital, and these young residents were not all that far removed from being students themselves. Most of them had an eye toward the future, when they themselves would be senior doctors and medical professors instructing students—students a lot like me. Some of them, I realize as I look back, were practicing their teaching on me. That was fine with me. I was soaking up everything I could about the doctors, their practice, and their patients. I felt like society at large was benefitting from the pharmaceutical products and knowledge I was bringing to the party. And, of course, it was never far from my mind that I was getting better and better at selling more of my pharmaceutical products and earning bigger salaries, commissions, and bonuses every year. I hung out with the doctors not only at the hospital but also outside. Sometimes they'd even take me out for beers.

By the time I was in my midforties, I had been with Carter-Wallace for 17 years, and I was one of the company's top-performing and top-earning sales reps for the entire country. For several years in a row I was Carter-Wallace's leading or No. 2 salesperson in the country for Felbatol, which was the leading drug for treating Lennox-Gastaut syndrome, a severe form of epilepsy that typically affects children under the age of five—the little kids you see wearing tiny fitted, padded helmets. When it came down to choosing a drug to treat epileptic patients, the doctors in Ohio, particularly those at the hospital in Cincinnati, increasingly prescribed Felbatol—my drug—as an anticonvulsant for Lennox-Gastaut syndrome. That was partly—a very small part—because they knew me and trusted me but mostly because Felbatol worked well.

The pharmacology of antiepileptic drugs can be complicated. Many antiepileptic drugs specify appropriate therapeutic "blood levels," a measure of the drug in the bloodstream. Blood levels for antiepileptic drugs can be very important because different drugs interact differently with different people and blood levels can vary widely from patient to patient, often indicating whether or when a certain drug is going to be effective or whether it is going to cause adverse reactions or even be dangerous to the patient. If someone has too much of the drug in his or her bloodstream or too little, the drug may not work properly, and the person may suffer side effects, possibly toxic. Blood levels in package insert materials are important. For example, let's say an epilepsy drug such as Dilantin, designed to reduce seizures, is indicated for a blood level of 10–20 micrograms per milliliter. If that drug is administered to a patient who shows a blood level above 20, the drug could be toxic—poisonous—and cause greater injury, illness, or even death.

For that same drug, a blood level of below 10 could increase the patient's seizures, which can also be life-threatening. Yes, we know different people respond differently to drugs and to different doses. The results of drugs can vary so much, patient to patient, and the stakes are so high—literally life and death. That's why the pharmaceutical industry is subject to so much testing and so many studies—and so many rules, like the prohibitions against off-label marketing.

Sometimes the package inserts, the directions for doctors in the drug packaging, do not include information on blood levels. Carter-Wallace knew that studies and drug trials showed that there was no distinct range of appropriate blood levels for Felbatol in most patients, and the FDA agreed. But Carter-Wallace was relying solely on the results of the drug trials that had been conducted on Felbatol before it was approved by the FDA for doctors to prescribe to the general public, and those preapproval drug trials can't catch every side effect or adverse reaction. Drug companies are supposed to keep track of side effects and adverse reactions that are discovered after the preapproval testing, when the drug is in actual use and being prescribed to the public.

A side effect may be rare enough that it doesn't show up in a preapproval trial of 350 patients. But the side effect may show up when the drug is prescribed to 100,000 actual patients. This is an "idiosyncratic reaction," a reaction that does not surface in clinical trials but does show up when used among many more real patients. That's what happened with Felbatol. The preapproval drug studies and trials that were approved by the FDA showed that there was no distinct range for blood levels. However, when Felbatol became widely prescribed, doctors began reporting that there could be bad side effects if the blood levels were too high. If a patient was given too much Felbatol, doctors prescribing the drug reported, the toxic adverse reactions could be aplastic anemia and hepatic or liver failure, both often fatal.

At one point, Dr. Smith at the hospital in Cincinnati, the one who was especially close to me, pulled me aside to talk about Felbatol. He noted that the package inserts from the FDA did not prescribe certain blood levels for Felbatol. "Hey, Bruce," he said. "Do you have blood levels on Felbatol?" I didn't hesitate. "No," I said. It was true. I had never received anything from my company indicating or recommending any specific blood levels, either high or low, for Felbatol. He nodded and seemed satisfied. I had reassured him, and he trusted me. When other doctors at the hospital also inquired about Felbatol's possible side effects and blood levels, I went back to the company and asked. Were there recommended drug levels? No, the company told me. No insert warnings were available or needed for Felbatol because there were no indications for problems with blood levels. I went back and told the doctors not to worry, that any potential—and very rare—side effects were not dependent on specific blood levels. The doctors all reacted the same way: OK, Bruce, great, thanks.

They trusted me.

But it wasn't true. There were potential problems with Felbatol's blood levels, and Carter-Wallace was not picking up on them and passing them along to its sales reps so that we could warn doctors and they could prescribe the drug more carefully. Tragically, it took the worst possible scenario—patients dying—for that to come to light.

During one of my visits to his office, Dr. Smith suggested that the next day I should come to grand rounds, the regular gatherings of a teaching hospital's staff physicians, residents, and medical students in a conference room or auditorium for a wide-ranging discussion about what they were seeing and learning in treating their patients. The "medical school model" of education is dependent on this kind of clinical research and sharing, and it can be very effective. It wasn't unusual for me to attend grand rounds. I had attended many times and loved it. I loved getting the latest information, and I loved rubbing shoulders with the doctors, hearing what they were hearing, and learning what they were learning. I felt like it made me better at my job and that the doctors wanted me there because they wanted me to be better at my job, too. "Sure," I said. "I'll be at grand rounds." I noted that he seemed unusually chilly toward me. He was distant. But I figured he must have something on his mind—maybe a patient in particular difficulty—and it had nothing to do with me.

"Good," he responded evenly. "I'm saving a seat for you right in front." That was unusual, and I was curious about it but figured he was simply giving me some special attention or a prime spot to get a good look at something he was going to reveal during his turn at the podium. Then he asked me the same question again about Felbatol: Did this drug have a specific therapeutic blood level? I said there were no particular dangers from blood levels with Felbatol. "Are you sure, Bruce?" he asked me. "Really sure?"

When I entered the auditorium for grand rounds, Dr. Smith nodded toward a vacant seat right in front, as promised. I sat down next to another guest, a young woman I had not seen before. When Dr. Smith's turn came at the podium, he introduced her as one of the hospital's patients. As an epileptic, she had been treated with Felbatol to control her seizures and had suffered a disastrous reaction—liver failure.

"She did not go into an epileptic seizure," the doctor told the other doctors. "No. Instead, she went straight into hepatic failure.

She was dying," he said and looked at me. "We're lucky we saved her life."

And it got worse. He went on to describe how a different Ohio hospital, in Columbus, had gone back and looked at other recent cases and determined that six other people, including two children, died from liver failure after being treated with Felbatol. The problem was the blood levels, he said. If the doctors at the hospital in Columbus had been told about the toxic risks to patients with inappropriate levels of Felbatol in their bloodstreams, those people might still be alive. The young woman seated next to me, treated by Dr. Smith at this hospital in Cincinnati, would not have nearly died. The doctors would have heeded the blood level warnings and not prescribed Felbatol. They would not have put their patients at risk.

Dr. Smith stared directly at me as he said all this. His voice was hard and even. His face was a bitter mask. I felt all the doctors in the room staring at me, too.

After grand rounds, everybody filed out without a word to me. Doctors who would have been talking and joking were stone-faced. They did not look at me. Nor did the young woman who had been seated next to me, the one who was lucky to be alive in spite of the drug that I had recommended to the doctors to control her epilepsy. The only person to speak to me was my doctor friend—my former friend now. He came straight up to me in the auditorium while everyone else was filing out. He got in my face. "Bruce, this is your drug. You should know better. You should have warned us. It's your drug, but she's our patient."

He wasn't finished with me. "This is on you and your company, Bruce," he told me. "This should not have happened."

He shook his head and said, as if to himself, "Lesson learned." I knew what lesson he had learned: not to befriend, work with, or trust a drug company representative, especially the one standing in front of him. I let him down. The worst part of it was that he no doubt thought I had misled him solely to make a little more money. Nothing could be further from the truth, but there was no way I would ever convince him of that. I slunk away. I was devastated. This was not what I envisioned for my life or my work.

My company's lack of attention to the dangers had caused deaths. The news about Felbatol—and Carter-Wallace's failure to warn doctors—spread through the medical community across Ohio and beyond. Doctors were calling us reps and saying, "Hey, what about this?" Carter-Wallace had to tell its sales reps to stop marketing Felbatol to doctors. The reps were told not to talk to anybody about Felbatol—not doctors, not hospitals, not patients, not government health officials, and not even other sales representatives. When Dr. Smith told me about the deaths, one of my most immediate thoughts was, "I have to leave this company. I can't work for Carter-Wallace anymore." I knew I could no longer be effective working for a company I didn't trust. I didn't want to work for a company that would be so haphazard and that would keep critical information about drug levels and side effects from sales reps like me.

Carter-Wallace told me, along with the other sales reps in neurology throughout the country, that we were being taken off neurology. We were being reassigned to general practices. No more teaching hospitals. At that stage in my career, after 17 years, it was a real professional comedown. Carter-Wallace didn't want other doctors confronting sales reps the way my doctor had confronted me. The company didn't want us sales reps talking about the company's negligence or saying anything else that could be used in lawsuits filed by patients—or their family members.

When Carter-Wallace disbanded the hospital sales force—the team I had been working on so happily for so long—it became easier to walk away. I got serious about my exit strategy. I wanted to find a company that would let me get back into neurology. It was what I knew and loved. My last weeks at Carter-Wallace, I was back in the office, driving around, office to office, talking to general practitioners about general practice concerns—the ailments that walked through the door every day. It was not nearly as interesting or inspiring as the challenges of neurology in a large teaching hospital. But leaving presented uncertainties. It was 1997, the American economy was booming, and so was my business at Carter-Wallace. Beth and I had a nice house, nice cars, a nice family. We had three growing kids.

Would I get a new job that would be as good for us?

Looking for a new job, I wanted to stay in Ohio, where I had deep family roots and where my life with Beth and the kids had always been centered. I still wanted to work in pharmaceutical sales. I was good at it. The work was rewarding, not only financially but also intellectually—when it was conducted in the right way.

I wanted to find a better company and do more of the good work I had been doing, helping doctors and their patients. I updated the résumé I had not used in 17 years and began quietly sending it out to other drug companies with operations in Ohio.

Six

Moving to Cephalon

*A*s word got out that I was looking to make a move, I began hearing from friends, colleagues, and acquaintances in the business. Their encouragement was really gratifying. Quite a few of them had suggestions for where I might apply, and several said I should come and work with them. One of those was John. He had been one of my colleagues, a sales rep like me at Carter-Wallace, before he left to take a higher-ranking job at Cephalon, a drug company that was expanding from research into manufacturing and sales. It was a sharp young company, John promised me, and I would love the emphasis on science and on doing things the right way.

Cephalon was started in Frazer, Pennsylvania, outside Philadelphia, by Frank Baldino, a pharmacologist, and two other scientists he had worked with for years at DuPont Co. Frank was the central figure, the chairman and CEO. The name for the company came from the word "cephalic," meaning related to the head or brain, and the company's goal was to concentrate on neurodegenerative diseases.

At first the company was pretty much a high-science company, doing research and clinical trials for other people's drugs. Its only asset was its scientific expertise, its only income from investors and research grants and payments from other drug companies for conducting trials. Eventually, though, Cephalon hired a sales force and began making and selling drugs itself, specializing in the treatment of headaches. Its best-known drug was Stadol, a "borrowed" drug acquired from Bristol-Myers Squibb. It might be a way back into neurology for me, I thought.

Frank Baldino, I learned, was a rising rock star in the pharmaceutical industry. I did my research on him—everyone I talked to said the same thing, and everything I read about him said it, too: He was the brilliant scientist, young and energetic, who also happened to be very smart about business. He was a born entrepreneur and a born leader. He was a cofounder but quickly became the dominant figure at Cephalon, the face and brains and heart of the company, a great motivator and inspiration.

My friend John called me in for an interview at Cephalon's headquarters in the suburbs of Philadelphia. Frank did not disappoint—he was a star scientist as well as an aggressive, ambitious, dynamic leader who had brilliant ideas and was a terrific motivator of people. Frank was dividing the United States into four sales areas, so he needed four area managers. At least that was Frank's original plan. I was afraid I might get assigned to a really big multistate area, but I convinced Frank that the company would get more sales by having me concentrate on Ohio, where everybody knew me and I knew everybody in the medical community, instead of spreading me out over 10 or more states. I was hired as a sales rep covering Ohio, Indiana, and part of Kentucky. I got a $65,000 salary and a $40,000 bonus, plus 10,000 shares in Cephalon. The shares back then were worth $2 each.

After I started with the company in 1997, my first year at Cephalon was a working dream, largely because I was able to plunge back into neurology. I came to develop a new appreciation, through Cephalon's drugs, for how neurology tackled the puzzles and the mysteries of treating ailments such as epilepsy and stroke. I was learning a lot again, building on what I had learned about neurology when I was with Carter-Wallace. I had by then overcome my dyslexia—or, rather, learned to live and work with it—to the point where I could read and absorb almost anything, including high-level studies and theories. Cephalon renewed the feeling that I had real empathy and the ability to help patients struggling with some of the conditions that caused them so much suffering. I also quickly developed a lot of new relationships with many of the doctors I served in my area. I again built up great reservoirs of trust with "my" doctors. In 1998, after about only a year at the company, I was promoted to Cephalon's Midwest area manager. I then had seven states and 12 people reporting to me. I also became a senior HR advisor because I was perceived as being good at interviewing job applicants. If the home office wanted a second interview with a candidate anywhere in the country, they'd fly me in to do it.

For my first three years at Cephalon, everything was great. I was happy selling mostly two drugs—the highly effective Provigil, the narcolepsy medication, which worked and which many doctors relied upon. It was an easy sell. I made sure the doctors I called on were aware of Gabitril, the other drug I handled, but with less success than Provigil. To many of Cephalon's sales reps, Gabitril was "a dog of a drug," largely ineffective and therefore not a good commission generator.

Cephalon was doing great. Frank was delivering on the science and the leadership. The 10,000 shares of Cephalon he gave me as a signing bonus back in 1997 were worth $85 each when I cashed them in years later. Between my savings and investments, I was a millionaire. Sometimes in a quiet moment, Beth and I would just look at each and start laughing. We couldn't believe it. It seemed like it wasn't that long ago we were a couple of poor kids trying to hold it all together—one struggling in a job he hated as the assistant manager of a sporting goods store, the other nearly overwhelmed with babies at home and who needed food, clothes, health care, and more. We were very lucky, we told ourselves.

Cephalon was a different sort of company from Carter-Wallace. Carter-Wallace had not been a high-science company, but it was a serious company, conservative to the point of being staid in many ways. Most of the other sales reps were older than me when I started working there, but I still felt like one of the younger people after being there 17 years. Carter-Wallace was the sort of place where people came to work and did their jobs and went home to their families. Nothing more, very little extra effort. Many stayed for decades. There weren't a lot of after-hours shenanigans.

Cephalon, in contrast, was a young company, with lots of young ambitious people who had not necessarily come up in the buttoned-down traditions of a conservative company like Carter-Wallace. Frank liked to hire people in his own image: smart, aggressive, sharp dressers, glib talkers—people who were always looking for an angle and a way to get on top. As one of the area managers, I was an exception. I had been in the business for years and was pushing 50. I was always one of the older, more established area managers on the Cephalon payroll.

The differences in the two companies became clearer as more young, aggressive, ambitious types joined Cephalon. People went out together after work. A lot. There was a great deal of drinking, especially at company sales meetings. The company seemed to be increasingly all about making money. People compared their numbers and seemed to be competing. I tried to stay above it all, and for the most part I could, since I was an area manager, a boss. I had an excuse for not carousing with everyone else. But I wasn't immune to ambition. Being an area manager had given me a taste of the executive life, and I liked it. I wanted more. At home, on the surface, it still seemed like everything was going great. I had stimulating work, made very good money, and had a happy family. But it wasn't as great as I thought, especially the happy family part. The kids were all good, and Beth and I rarely argued. But after more than two decades, things were different between us. We were complacent. We weren't as interested in each other as we had been.

Looking back, I suppose we took each other for granted. We were both at fault—or, rather, we were each at fault but in different ways. My work gave me so much satisfaction. There was so much that was new and different every day, so many exciting challenges, new products, new calls to make, new people to meet and win over, both to me personally and to Cephalon's products. I loved overseeing the sales reps under me, in my area, keeping track of them, helping them when I could, guiding them when they let me. It was very satisfying. I was getting a lot of recognition from the company, including awards and bonuses, for the numbers my team and I put up.

I was so busy that there was never enough time for everything I had to do at work—which spilled over into my home life. Sometimes it was easier to spend more time and energy on work than on my family. Beth would always be OK, I told myself; she didn't need me around all the time. But she needed me around more than I was there for her. And I needed to be paying for the house and the cars and the next big scuba diving trip for the family.

Beth didn't see it quite that way. She missed me. She might have been satisfied for me to still be running a sporting goods store, if not for the money. She liked it when I was the husband who came home at the same time for dinner every evening and the dad who went to all the kids' games and practices. She didn't like me being away so much—the nights out of town on the road, the sales dinners, the professional conferences. She would have loved for me to come home for lunch. As my career progressed, I was away from home more. I was called on more frequently for higher-level meetings anywhere in the country.

When it became increasingly clear that Cephalon was grooming me for higher management, I was pleased. I wanted to keep moving, onward and upward, grabbing the next brass ring. I remember when Cephalon needed an area manager to attend a conference and set up FDA guidelines for leaving free samples of controlled substances with doctors' offices. I was asked to do it, and I was flattered. It was a big deal, high profile, important for the company.

My guidelines were a big success, and I got a lot of praise from the bosses and respect from the sales reps around the country. One year in the late 1990s when I was honored for my national sales performance, the company flew Beth and me to the Bahamas for a conference to receive Cephalon's President's Award, the company's top honor. On that trip, Beth and I had the first really big fight of our more than 20 years together as a couple.

She wanted me to step off the fast track. She especially wanted me to turn down Cephalon's entreaties for me to become a higher-ranking executive. I couldn't understand it. Wasn't this what we had been working so hard for all these years? No, as it turned out. That is what I wanted, not what Beth wanted.

We couldn't understand each other. She couldn't understand how a career, how a job, could compete with spending more time with her and our kids. I couldn't understand what I saw as her lack of appreciation for my hard work, my professional progress, and the kind of provider I had become for the family. Couldn't we have both? We tried, for several years, the best we could. Beth finally asked me for a divorce in 2000. It wasn't a happy divorce—what divorce really is?—but we did our best to be civil to each other and to take care of the kids. It was tough for both of us sometimes. Neither of us could understand why the other was doing this to the family. But we came through it, somehow, as still each other's best friend.

We've come to recognize who we are and to respect each other for who we are. We tried to change each other, and it didn't work. But we still needed to raise the kids together in a civil manner, in a manner that would be best for them. And we did that. And we emerged from the whole thing—marriage, divorce, raising the kids, and getting them launched—with a remarkably strong friendship based on that shared history. She's done some amazing things for me over the years, especially during my tough times as a whistleblower. I've tried to do good things for her, too, but it will never be enough to make up for everything she's given me in life, starting with those three kids.

Seven

Using Doctors for Off-Label Promotion

*D*octors sometimes come to realize that a drug that is supposed to do one thing might also or instead do something else for some patients. They recognize that the use of drugs can evolve as they become more commonly prescribed. It is entirely permissible for a doctor to prescribe an antiseizure epilepsy drug for a mood disorder instead—provided it works and doesn't cause any harmful side effects. Doctors can do that. But drug company reps cannot legally promote or sell drugs for off-label purposes. As a sales rep, I was not allowed to get into a physician's office and say, "Hey, doc, I know that epilepsy drug isn't working very well for your patients, but it works really well for a lot of people with mood disorders. Want a free sample? Try it on some patients."

No, I could not do that. That was "selling off-label," and it was illegal for pharmaceutical sales reps.

However, any doctor can write off-label. And many doctors will happily do that—if they have some good information or advice that the drug, off-label, will work for their patients—even if it is prescribed for something other than intended, something that is not on the label, something the FDA has not approved.

But how do doctors get that information or advice? Well, they can get it from other doctors, in medical journals or at conferences or even on the golf course. But how do those other doctors know to try a drug off-label? What spurs that first doctor, for example, to prescribe a drug that is designated for treating one condition or disease for something totally different? Sometimes when a drug has been widely prescribed for a medical condition that is not indicated—approved—in the package inserts, it seems to work for this unintended purpose.

When that happens, the pharmaceutical companies producing the drug often fund studies to show that it really does work, and there is some scientific basis for adding a new indication to the package insert. Sometimes doctors hear or read about these studies, and sometimes the FDA itself changes and expands the indications for the drug.

But even without additional studies, doctors often get information and advice about prescribing drugs off-label, for unintended purposes—from the same sources they get much of the rest of their information and advice about prescription drugs—from the pharmaceutical sales reps who call on them in their offices.

Yes, again, it is illegal for sales reps to recommend to doctors that any drug be prescribed off-label. But there are ways around the rules. Sometimes, one-on-one in the doctors' offices, with no witnesses, a doctor and sales rep will have a conversation that is very direct about using a certain drug off-label. They both know that conversation is forbidden, and they both understand they can never admit to having that conversation. But it can serve both of them. For the doctor, the recommendation of a trusted pharmaceutical company rep—and many doctors trust their longtime reps implicitly—saves hours of time on researching medications and smooths the way for better treatment of patients. That's everyone's goal, of course: better treatment of patients.

But relying on a sales rep for smart, effective recommendations can also make a doctor's job easier, freeing up the doctor's time for other medical or office duties. Or it can free up more personal time for the doctor. For the sales rep, a good off-label medication recommendation that gains a doctor's trust can mean it is easier for that sales rep to persuade the doctor to try something else the rep's pharmaceutical company is offering, especially new drugs that a doctor might otherwise be reluctant to try.

One of the ways sales reps can get around the federal regulations against selling off-label is by simply leaving information, typically copies of printed articles, in the doctor's office, maybe on the doctor's desk. The drug companies argue that their sales reps have a First Amendment right to leave that information where a doctor will find it and read it. The reasoning is free speech—the

First Amendment bars the government from restricting free speech—and the drug rep, at least in the drug rep's view and the drug company's view, is exercising the right of free speech by leaving a doctor something that claims a drug can and should be used for some medical treatment other than its intended and approved use.

My lawyer, Peter Chatfield, would later explain this interpretation of the law, saying, "Truthful communication of genuine information about a drug and its scientifically supported potential benefits in off-label uses is protected by the First Amendment. But the government is entitled to require that such communications be done in a way that protects against unlawful inducements and exaggerated claims of safety or efficacy. The government has been careful to limit its enforcement actions to conduct that pretty clearly involves unlawful inducements and/ or misrepresentation of the scientific support for efficacy and/or inaccurate representation of safety considerations."

The US Supreme Court first extended commercial speech free speech protection in 1975. Previously, it had been applied only to individuals and especially for political speech. Several rulings in the mid seventies, though, opened the door for business advertisements and corporate promotional materials to be protected under the amendment, provided that the claims were accurate and legal.

Most sales reps don't question the ethics or legality of off-label sales. Many do it quietly, without a lot of attention from their bosses, let alone the authorities. That's what happened at Cephalon in the late 1990s and early 2000s. I don't know which of my colleagues started selling Cephalon drugs off-label, but it started happening, and more and more reps started doing it. We'd get together at sales meetings or conferences, and nothing official was said—at least for a while—but the sales reps who were making extra money by selling off-label were soon giving the rest of us the heads-up. "Hey, have you guys heard about this?" I remember the first time I heard this conversation was at a sales meeting in California when I was an area manager. The reps who had started selling off-label explained how they told doctors that this one drug for treating X can also be used to effectively treat Y. It didn't seem like a big deal to them. The rest of us could see that the reps who were selling off-label were getting great results—their numbers were up. Everybody wanted their numbers to go up. Everybody wanted to make more money. So everybody tried it. Including me. Not right away but eventually and not for long.

For a couple of years, the sales reps at Cephalon increasingly sold off-label for a small number of medications. I have no doubt that Frank and the company's other top executives knew what was going on, but they looked the other way. They liked the results. Sales were up. The company's stock price was climbing, so shareholders were happy. The bonuses for the executives were going up, so they were happy. When I was interviewing for a new job after leaving Carter-Wallace, Cephalon did not seem like a company that had any ingrained ethical issues. Off-label sales were not a concern—not even mentioned during my interview and hiring process. During my five years at the company, selling off-label came to be not merely quietly accepted at Cephalon but part of the business model.

I think the move toward off-label marketing at Cephalon had roots in something that happened around the time I joined the company in 1997. Cephalon had developed a promising new drug to treat ALS, the degenerative condition commonly known as Lou Gehrig's disease. There is no cure for ALS, which affects nerve cells in the brain and spinal cord, and Frank never said there was. But he believed this new drug, Myotrophin, could slow the process of mental and physical decline for the estimated 5,600 people a year diagnosed with ALS and perhaps extend the lives of sufferers by months or years and enrich their well-being with the ability to still enjoy friends, family, and life in general.

Frank was not trying to promote Myotrophin off-label; it had not even been approved for prescription sales yet. But the FDA thought Frank was overselling it, that he was claiming and promising that the drug could do more to slow ALS than it really could. The FDA put Cephalon and Myotrophin through a wringer of studies and trials, and for a time Frank put up with it all, smiling but gritting his teeth, saying all the right things publicly but cursing at the FDA in private. The costs of all the studies and trials kept adding up, to the point that the investment in Myotrophin did not make sense given the relatively small number of ALS sufferers—an estimated 30,000 Americans.

Frank never could understand why the FDA was making it so difficult. Yes, he agreed, maybe Myotrophin was not a cure-all for every one of those 30,000 ALS patients, but it might help some of them. It wasn't going to cure anyone. It wasn't going to extend every patient's life by years—but it might extend some patients' lives by months. Frank really believed Myotrophin could make a difference for some patients with ALS in their last years and months with the disease.

Myotrophin also had a lot of fans, including the national ALS Association, which lobbied the FDA for years to approve the drug, including through a letter-writing campaign by ALS patients, their families, and survivors. Frank had a meeting with the FDA's people supervising drugs related to the central nervous system, including any drugs to treat ALS. That meeting did not go well for Frank or Cephalon or Myotrophin. He ended up railing at the FDA staffers and all but ending the chances of Myotrophin getting approval.

Myotrophin was never approved by the FDA for treating ALS or anything else. Frank blamed the FDA for keeping a potentially helpful drug from suffering patients who really needed some help—and for keeping him and Cephalon from a financial recovery in the form of corporate profits. By the time Cephalon pulled the plug on Myotrophin, the company had spent close to $200 million developing and testing the drug—for zero return. Frank regarded the FDA as not only an annoyance but also a stumbling block to better drugs and better business.

The FDA was an irritant, and after the Myotrophin debacle, he ignored the FDA whenever and however he could.

From a few Cephalon drug reps promoting the company's drugs off-label on their own, without Cephalon's knowledge or permission, it became clear that the company did know. Nothing was done by the company to object or do anything to stop reps from selling off-label. Next, it became that clear the company was giving tacit approval, with a wink and a nod to reps who were selling Cephalon's drugs off-label, illegally, for unintended purposes. Most reps, it should be noted, didn't mind selling off-label, even though some of them acknowledged to me, privately, that it felt wrong somehow to be selling off-label, without the company's permission. By the time I was pushed out in 2003, Cephalon sales reps were being trained to sell off-label—illegally—even though it wasn't acknowledged. A sales rep who admitted marketing drugs off-label would be fired. But a sales rep who didn't market Cephalon's drugs off-label would not meet the sales targets the company had set. It was impossible to meet the sales targets and get a bonus without quietly marketing the company's drugs off-label. "You gotta be able to play in the gray area," the company sales trainers told us.

Frank and the other top Cephalon executives characterized selling off-label as our duty and responsibility, not only to the company and to our families but also to our doctors and their patients and to the medical profession in general. If a drug would work, whether for its intended purpose or not, we had a right and a duty to get it out there. The Cephalon executives added one wrinkle that had not occurred to me. Under FDA rules, if a drug is used off-label long enough and widely enough—presumably at the instigation of a doctor, which would be legal, instead of a drug rep, which would be illegal—the FDA could consider the results and change the indications for that drug. The unintended purpose could be officially included, if it worked, as one of the official, intended purposes.

Frank Baldino and other Cephalon reps set about institutionalizing off-label sales throughout the company. They set up training sessions for sales reps, showing us how to do it. They recruited sales agents from other companies who didn't see any problem with going off-label. They helped the sales reps target certain doctors who were most likely to be persuaded to prescribe off-label. The company recruited doctors not only to write prescriptions for but also to speak in favor of specific off-label sales. Some doctors were happy to talk up the joys of using a certain drug for other purposes in relatively casual conversations over steak dinners in a nice restaurant with a few other doctors from their town. "Peer group selling," it was called.

Doctors who talked up off-label prescribing liked being the center of attention among their peers. They liked it when other doctors listened to them and sought their advice. They weren't making promises, after all; they were merely alerting their colleagues to something that might work. If it worked, great. If it didn't, well, it was worth a try. It was good for doctors, for their egos, for their standing, and often for their business. It was good for them when they got their names out there and when they enhanced their reputations as physicians with patients, with other doctors who might give them referrals, and with drug companies that might pay them more in the future to become spokespersons for their drugs.

But the status and prestige among other doctors were side benefits. I am convinced that money was the main motivating factor for most of the doctors who conspired with Cephalon to promote drugs off-label. Some doctors were paid writing fees for producing articles that the company may have had written for them to put their names on. Some doctors got speaking fees for going to medical conferences and giving talks on how to use one drug for something else and how it really worked. One doctor, I know, routinely got $1,500 speaking for 15 minutes at luncheons. That's $100 a minute, and that was on the low end of the consulting scale for doctors who were helping spread the word that some drugs could be used effectively for other, unapproved purposes. A few doctors got vacations to resorts or aboard cruise ships for speaking at meetings to preach the gospel of Cephalon and off-label prescriptions. Some doctors spoke three times a day— breakfast, lunch, and dinner—for 15 minutes each and collected $1,500 for each talk, a total of $4,500 for the day. Honorariums, consulting fees, speaking fees, gifts—however you characterize it, a fair amount of money flowed from Cephalon to doctors who were willing to encourage other doctors to join them in writing more prescriptions of Cephalon products. Medicine is historically one of the best-paid professions in America, and some of these doctors were earning a significant share of their total annual income directly from Cephalon and other drug companies they were willing to promote. I'm convinced that one doctor in particular was paid hundreds of thousands of dollars over a very few years to train other doctors to help promote Cephalon's off-label marketing. On the face of it, paying a doctor $1,500 for a luncheon designed to facilitate peer group selling may have seemed like a significant expense. A big fancy lunch plus $4,500 to get three doctors to attend and talk up off-label sales? That was a small investment for Cephalon for the returns it was getting from off-label sales. Those expenses were more than worth the return.

Was any of this illegal on the part of doctors? Probably not. Cephalon and the doctors could claim they had a normal, run-of-the-mill consulting arrangement, with the doctors providing time and expertise and the company paying them for it. Cephalon's sales reps, not the doctors, were breaking the law through off-label marketing.

Eight

Gabitril & Provigil Goes Off-Label

*J*ohn, my longtime friend and ally within the company, the former Carter-Wallace colleague who had recruited me for Cephalon, wanted to talk to me. He wanted to make sure I was aware that one of the neurology drugs I handled was being marketed off-label by a different sales team. I wasn't aware. I was surprised and a little shocked when John told me that the pain division was marketing Gabitril, the not-very-effective anticonvulsant intended to treat epilepsy, for an entirely different purpose. He said the Cephalon pain team was promoting Gabitril not to prevent seizures but to ease anxiety and neuropathic pain.

This was wrong. It was blatant off-label marketing, a clear violation of FDA rules. Nowhere did anything in the Gabitril package inserts say that this drug was effective for pain relief.

There had been no tests, no studies, no evidence. Cephalon had been selling Gabitril for several years, and it had sold well at first. Lots of doctors treating epileptics were willing to give it a chance as an antiseizure drug. Cephalon's sales team marketed it to doctors as a drug that could keep seizures from happening and make them less severe and easier to control among patients who still have seizures.

Gabitril sold pretty well in 1999 and 2000, but then its fortunes started waning. It simply didn't work that well, or at least not as well as Cephalon's sales reps promised. It worked sometimes, for some patients, but not often enough or well enough to be a go-to drug for doctors to prescribe. As sales and commissions declined, Cephalon's sales reps not only began muttering that Gabitril was "a dog of a drug" but also called it "Gabawater" for its lack of effectiveness. Cephalon's sales reps wished that they had something better to offer, something that sold better—something that made more money for us and might be a better drug. Or, in this case, it might be an old drug that was suddenly being used for new and different purposes—and turned out to be highly effective for new and different purposes.

That's what happened with Gabitril. Cephalon's sales reps began spreading the word among their doctors: instead of for seizures, try prescribing Gabitril for anxiety or neuropathic issues—including the vague, hard-to-diagnose, hard-to-pinpoint chronic nervous system pain that many Americans began complaining about in the late twentieth century. How did this start? Who first got the idea that Gabitril might work for this unintended purpose? I don't think we'll ever know that. But it was a great sales strategy, filling a gap in the market. At that time, many in the medical community were puzzling over mysterious patient complaints about various types of pain.

Doctors were looking for anything that might help, and when Cephalon's drug reps said Gabitril might help, some doctors tried prescribing it to patients. Gabitril worked for some of them—or at least they said it did. Some reported to their doctors that they felt less anxious. Some reported that their vague pain was not as bad after taking Gabitril. How many of these people were truly helped by Gabitril—and how many were benefiting from the placebo effect—can never be known. But we do know that some people developed side effects when they stopped taking Gabitril—including seizures. People who had never had epilepsy were taking Gabitril off-label for anxiety or neuropathic pain; when Gabitril didn't work or stopped working, patients could potentially start suffering seizures for the first time in their lives.

It soon became clear that a great many of Cephalon's sales reps were pitching Gabitril to doctors off-label—including the reps who worked for me. I talked to them about it, and they didn't seem to think there was anything wrong with selling Gabitril for anxiety and neuropathic pain. If it worked, they reasoned, why not? They were more reluctant to point out that it was putting more money in their pockets, but that was clearly a major factor. "My numbers are up," one of them told me, ending our conversation. None of my sales reports had heard anything about bad side effects, like seizures for people who were not epileptics.

Nor had I. My sales reps told me I should be selling off-label, too. The company had been quietly encouraging them, they told me—even if I hadn't.

I thought about it and wasn't sure I wanted to go down that road. I just wasn't sure that selling off-label was right—or whether it was right for me. Then one day, in the office of one of my favorite physicians, the doctor told me—again—about a patient, a woman in her early forties, who had suddenly developed unexplained pain that came and went throughout her body. She thought it was fibromyalgia. The doctor didn't know whether that's what it was, but he didn't know what else it could be, either. He just wanted to help her. And now she was becoming increasingly anxious about her health. She was getting depressed because she was so easily exhausted and because she so quickly developed pain, especially in her extremities.

Sometimes, after trying to do just a little bit of work in the house or out in the garden, she felt like her arms and legs were on fire, and she suddenly became so tired she could barely make it to bed, where she sobbed in pain, trying to go to sleep. It wasn't an unusual story. He had a number of patients who were suffering from some similar condition, and many of my other doctors did, too. This doctor, on this day, brought up using Gabitril for anxiety. Other doctors had been talking about it, and some of them said it helped some patients. "You know anything about that?" the doctor asked me.

Cephalon had instructed its sales reps, if asked, to be positive about Gabitril as a pain reliever. I tried, as always, to play it straight. I told him what my sales reps had been telling me; yes, Gabitril did seem to help some patients suffering from what seemed like fibromyalgia but could not be definitively diagnosed. I used the term "off-label" with the doctor, knowing that he knew what off-label was. He was not fazed. "I think I want to try it for this patient," he said. "What do you think?"

I said OK and that I would arrange for his office to receive some free samples to offer this patient and any other patients he thought might be helped by Gabitril. And so I was selling off-label, too, even though I felt in my heart it was wrong. The same sort of scenario played out a few more times, but I was never comfortable with it, even when it was a doctor, and not me, bringing it up.

Gabitril got off to a fast start as an off-label drug for anxiety and neuropathic pain; lots of doctors prescribed it because we drug reps made it sound so good. But patients soon reported no improvement, and doctors stopped prescribing it. Gabitril crashed and burned in the marketplace. Again.

After turning a blind eye and allowing sales reps to market Gabitril off-label on their own, Cephalon's leadership realized the potential of off-label marketing. They decided that a more organized but still under-the-radar approach to marketing other drugs off-label could be not only profitable but also sustainable. I soon became aware that Cephalon was marketing two other drugs off-label, Provigil and Actiq, in addition to Gabitril. Provigil, which I knew well and had been marketing successfully to many doctors for years, is a stimulant designed to treat narcolepsy.

Cephalon was promoting it off-label for sleepiness among multiple sclerosis patients, and it was apparently working well. Provigil was also being marketed off-label for patients who were depressed and had issues with sleepiness.

Provigil was designed to treat narcolepsy, the so-called sleeping sickness that some regard as something of a joke—what's so bad about falling asleep? It's kind of funny, after all, falling asleep at work or in class or in a conversation. Narcolepsy is no joke, though, if you're one of the estimated 125,000 Americans suffering from it. It's not so funny if you're the one who is having trouble in class or at work or if you're dozing off at the wheel or can't keep your eyes open when you're out on a date or having a serious conversation with a loved one.

People with narcolepsy can feel sidelined, isolated, and ostracized. They're not part of normal life. People with narcolepsy can become depressed. Unlike Gabitril, which didn't work very well or sell very well, we sales reps regarded Provigil as a "good drug," one of the best advances in the treatment of narcolepsy in decades. It was extremely effective in helping people with narcolepsy stay awake during the daytime and sleep at night. Provigil was changing the lives of patients for the better—and, since it was the go-to drug for many doctors, it was making solid money for Cephalon's sales reps.

Provigil was prescribed largely through sleep centers. Sleep centers typically have a large percentage of patients suffering from narcolepsy. Doctors began noticing that some people treated with Provigil for narcolepsy were reporting that they felt less depressed, too. Their moods were better. Their depression lifted as they took Provigil and as their narcolepsy eased. Instead of falling asleep at inopportune and inappropriate times during the day and then not being able to sleep at night, patients were staying awake all day and sleeping more soundly throughout the night. Naturally, their lives improved dramatically. Was it because of the Provigil or because they were sleeping better? Or both?

Not long after Provigil was first marketed off-label to neurologists for MS fatigue patients, Cephalon seized on the fact that psychiatrists are among the high-volume prescribers of antidepression medicine. The company began instructing its sales reps to suggest to psychiatrists that Provigil could also be used to augment depression therapy. Some psychiatrists prescribed for patients who tried it and reported good results. Provigil seemed to help with depression whether or not the patient suffered from narcolepsy. Word spread, and before long quite a few psychiatrists—and other doctors, too—were prescribing Provigil for augmentation of depression therapy. Before being treated with Provigil, some patients had not only suffered from depression but also complained about feeling drowsy all day. They weren't falling asleep uncontrollably, like the people suffering from classic narcolepsy, but they were tired all day and had trouble focusing and stayed focused. Some doctors reasoned that if Provigil could help people with narcolepsy stay awake, maybe it could also help these folks who were drowsy all day. A few doctors prescribed it off-label for a few patients, and it worked for some of them. They weren't drowsy. They could stay mentally sharp and on task for longer periods of time. Word spread among doctors, and pretty soon Cephalon was routinely peddling Provigil not only for narcolepsy and not only for depression but also as a concentration drug.

Then we heard about some studies that bolstered the claims that Provigil could help patients who were trying to be more alert and more attentive and who wanted to think better. They wanted to be smarter longer and not get tired. One study of Air Force pilots was very influential. The Air Force study showed that Provigil kept pilots alert and enhanced their awareness. It seemed to help them stay cognitively sharper for longer periods. The pilots were thinking more clearly under pressure, recognizing different situations more quickly, and making the right decisions more effectively. This opened up a whole new universe of eager patients for off-label Provigil prescriptions. It became a go-to medication for college students pulling all-nighters, fighter pilots, air traffic controllers, and others who had to stay totally focused for long periods of time without getting weary. Who doesn't need to stay on task? Who doesn't need a pick-me-up once in a while when doing a repetitive but demanding task? Cephalon encouraged doctors to prescribe Provigil for these new, unapproved, unintended purposes. "Yeah, military pilots love it," our sales reps told doctors. "College kids are getting into it for studying, for pulling all-nighters. Long-haul truckers, too. Here are some free samples, doc." OK, doctors said, let's try it on a few patients. It helped that Provigil really did work in increasing alertness for many people.

But Provigil had side effects, potentially deadly adverse reactions. The most common and least dangerous adverse reactions were headache, anxiety, nausea, and trouble sleeping—no surprise for a narcolepsy drug. Less common but more dangerous consequences included hallucinations and severe allergic reactions, such as anaphylaxis, the potentially fatal reaction that can come on within seconds. Within the general population, it's best known for the danger to people who are severely allergic to peanuts or bee stings. Perhaps the most extreme adverse reaction was Stevens-Johnson syndrome, a horrifying skin reaction that literally kills your skin. It can start with a fever and flu-like symptoms, followed within days by blisters as the skin dies. The blisters and dead skin peel away, leaving sore, raw patches. Patients can become dehydrated, and the mucous membranes in the mouth can dry up. Infections and pneumonia can follow and, ultimately, multiple organ failure. To my knowledge, Cephalon reps marketing Provigil off-label were not mentioning any of these side effects, including Stevens-Johnson syndrome, to their doctors.

As with Gabitril, sales of Provigil shot up with Cephalon's off-label marketing. Unlike Gabitril, however, Provigil was an effective drug for a large majority of the patients who took it, and its sales continued to grow.

When I experimented with selling off-label, I didn't feel like I was selling my soul. It didn't seem like the doctors were making a deal with the devil. It seemed like we were all trying to do what was best for everybody. Here was a drug that might help this particular patient—should we not try it because of some arcane fine-print rules in a government agency in Washington, DC? Or should we bust through the red tape and try to help the patient? Wasn't that what we were supposed to be doing: the doctor as a healer and the sales rep as part of the doctor's support team? It seemed like selling off-label was good for everybody—doctor, patient, and, oh yeah, the sales rep who would be bringing home a considerably fatter check at the end of the month.

I saw my month-end numbers go up during the brief period when I tried going off-label with a few doctors for Provigil. But selling off-label never felt right. I kept thinking back to Cincinnati, when I had not been careful enough and had encouraged neurologists to prescribe Felbatol without knowing exactly what the blood levels should be. I couldn't forget the way the young doctor spoke to me, or the young woman sitting next to me at grand rounds who had almost died, or the six people who did die. Selling off-label drugs now, knowingly, felt just as bad to me—or worse, since I knew that I was pushing a drug for a treatment that it was not supposed to be used for.

I stopped selling off-label. Doctors who were using Gabitril off-label could keep doing it if they wanted to. I stopped telling other doctors about it, but I didn't try to persuade any doctors prescribing Gabitril to stop. It's not supposed to be a drug rep's job to tell doctors how to prescribe or what not to prescribe. We provide information, and doctors decide. Maybe I could have provided more information about potential side effects, but it seemed presumptuous. Thankfully, I never heard about any of my team's patients suffering from any of the worst side effects of Provigil or Gabitril. That was not true of other company sales reps and the third drug Cephalon was marketing off-label. That drug turned out to be a lot more dangerous and with more widespread negative impact than the other two drugs put together. It became part of the opioid crisis in America.

Nine

The Opioid Lollipop— ER on a Stick

*T*he third neurology product Cephalon promoted off-label, in addition to Gabitril and Provigil, was Actiq, a powerful and dangerous drug for very specific, limited pain related to very serious cancer cases. Instead of being limited to use for cancer pain, however, Actiq was being sold off-label by Cephalon for all sorts of pain that it was never intended to treat, especially low-back pain and migraine headaches. Cephalon acquired Actiq after taking over the smaller pharmaceuticals company that had developed it. Actiq is an opioid—one of the first opioid brands and one of the most powerful. Its active ingredient is fentanyl, an especially dangerous opioid, 100 times as powerful as morphine.

Opioids had been around for years, dating back to the 1960s, but were not widely used or understood. Now, suddenly, a few doctors saw opioids as a new and better and more effective way of managing pain. Little-known fentanyl turned out to be the most effective—and perhaps most deadly—of all the opioid drugs. Remember that this off-label marketing was happening in the early 2000s, well before the opioid epidemic ravaged America, before tens of thousands of people died of overdoses, before addiction tore apart millions of families, before school kids were routinely writing term papers about opioids. Again, as with the other drugs Cephalon was marketing off-label, doctors were not being warned by sales reps about the side effects of Actiq, including addiction and death. Indeed, it wasn't until several years later that the FDA began investigating the dangers of fentanyl.

Here's some background on opioids from the federal government's National Institute on Drug Abuse:

In the late 1990s, pharmaceutical companies reassured the medical community that patients would not become addicted to prescription opioid pain relievers, and health-care providers began to prescribe them at greater rates. This subsequently led to widespread diversion and misuse of these medications before it became clear that these medications could indeed be highly addictive. Opioid overdose rates began to increase. In 2017, more than 47,000 Americans died as a result of an opioid overdose, including prescription opioids, heroin, and illicitly manufactured fentanyl, a powerful synthetic opioid. That same year, an estimated 1.7 million people in the United States suffered from substance use disorders related to prescription opioid pain relievers, and 652,000 suffered from a heroin use disorder (not mutually exclusive).

The federal Centers for Disease Control and Prevention tracks the epidemic of opioid deaths in three distinct waves:

1. *The first wave began with increased prescribing of opioids in the 1990s, with overdose deaths involving prescription opioids (natural and semi-synthetic opioids and methadone) increasing since at least 1999.*
2. *The second wave began in 2010, with rapid increases in overdose deaths involving heroin.*
3. *The third wave began in 2013, with significant increases in overdose deaths involving synthetic opioids—particularly those involving illicitly-manufactured fentanyl (IMF). The IMF market continues to change, and IMF can be found in combination with heroin, counterfeit pills, and cocaine.*

Beginning in 1998, Cephalon had approval to market Actiq for "breakthrough" cancer pain, the kind of searing, unbearable pain that other drugs cannot dim or dull. It's the kind of pain that breaks through all the usual medication. It is unbearable pain from the type of cancer that destroys a human body from the inside. The FDA was very specific, according to legal documents: Actiq was to be used only for cancer patients "with malignancies who are already receiving and who are tolerant to opioid therapy for their underlying persistent cancer pain."

When nothing else worked, when no other prescription painkillers helped dim the pain anymore, doctors could prescribe Actiq to cancer patients, usually patients in or near the end stages of their struggle. These were typically patients suffering horribly. Actiq was, for many doctors and their patients, the last straw, the final hope of easing their suffering. For many, Actiq was the only hope of enduring the last stages of cancer without constant pain—the kind of pain most of us cannot imagine. The term "breakthrough pain" was not a well-known medical description. Interestingly enough, it was invented by Cephalon's marketing people specifically to help sell Actiq.

Actiq proved quite effective for its designed purpose of easing breakthrough cancer pain. It was regarded by sales reps as a good drug, but it was not a huge moneymaker for them because it was basically a "hospital" drug. General practitioners or clinicians rarely prescribed it. It was primarily marketed to and prescribed by hospital oncologists, doctors who were treating cancer patients who were suffering the most and probably had little time left. Actiq was used primarily to help make those patients' last days a little more bearable. "The FDA also required that Actiq be provided only in compliance with a strict risk-management program that explicitly limited the drug's direct marketing to the approved target audiences, which was defined as oncologists, pain specialists, their nurses and office staff," according to legal documents.

Cephalon bridled under the FDA rules that sharply restricted who could prescribe Actiq and who could take it. Those restrictions meant that Actiq sales were restricted, too—only $15 million in 2000—with little chance of significant growth. And Cephalon was all about growth, which meant selling more.

To boost sales, Cephalon ignored the FDA rules and the restrictions and warnings on Actiq package inserts. Instead of concentrating solely on oncologists treating severe cancer pain and aiming prescriptions at breakthrough pain, Cephalon went off-label with Actiq and began talking to neurologists, anesthesiologists, pain doctors, and even general practitioners about how it could work for migraines and other headaches, back pain, sports injuries. It was an easy sell.

Reps could tell doctors, "Hey, you've got patients with chronic pain? The kind of intense pain that is ruining their lives? Why don't you try this medicine that is meant for cancer patients?"

Doctors listened, accepted what the drug reps were saying about Actiq, and prescribed it. It helped a lot of patients—provided the doctors strictly limited the strength and frequency of the prescriptions and the patients were not taking doses that were too strong. Many patients, particularly migraine patients, said it eased their pain. Before long, however, even patients taking modest doses of Actiq found themselves craving their next dose and begging their doctors to renew and strengthen their prescriptions.

Company documents later indicated that Cephalon told its sales reps not to bother calling on cancer doctors, the ones who were supposed to be prescribing Actiq. Instead, given the early enthusiasm among patients getting off-label prescriptions, Cephalon was ordering its sales reps to concentrate on doctors who might write prescriptions for migraine pain—there were a lot more people complaining about migraine pain than breakthrough cancer pain.

Studies cited in legal documents allege that visits by Cephalon sales reps to non-oncologists—who were not supposed to be visited at all—increased sixfold between 2002 and 2005. Cephalon often handed out dozens of coupons for free samples of Actiq with each visit; from today's perspective, that compares to the neighborhood pusher handing out free samples on the playground in order to get new customers. Within two years Actiq sales nearly doubled, and within five years sales had increased from $15 million to more than $400 million. By 2005, Actiq's sales total had jumped to $412 million. By then, only 1 percent of the prescriptions for Actiq being filled at retail pharmacies had been written by oncologists, according to legal documents, and a survey indicated that four out of five Actiq patients did not have cancer at all. All this, remember, for a drug that the FDA said should be prescribed for only a small group of cancer patients, those with "breakthrough pain."

It's easy to say, well, that was a long time ago, and we didn't know much about opioids. But I think we did know how dangerous opioids were. Or we should have, if we had looked at what opioids actually do. But here's the thing with Actiq and with fentanyl in general. It was administered in tiny doses, slowly—via a thin coating on a lollipop. It wasn't a real lollipop, but it was designed to look like one and to be used like one. The lollipop had a very thin coating of fentanyl. It was a "transmucosal" drug, designed to be absorbed through the membranes and mucous of the mouth, bypassing the liver. Properly administered, as in Cephalon's lollipop, a dose of fentanyl as small as two milligrams—that would fit on the head of a pin—can be fatal. If you are suffering from a fentanyl overdose, it becomes difficult and then impossible to breathe. Organs begin shutting down. The heart fails. There have been reports of people dying from merely touching fentanyl, not even ingesting it.

Despite the dangers, Cephalon passed along little in the way of warnings to sales reps or, indirectly, to doctors. Instead, the company made a big fuss over Actiq as a pain cure-all. Frank Baldino got a lot of publicity, as the company's glamor-boy CEO, for saying there was no downside to Actiq. He called it "ER on a stick."

But Actiq was still an opioid. It was still powerful and still dangerous. Some patients became addicted. Some of them overdosed. It took years for authorities to add up the deaths and blame them on Actiq—including, over time, 56 patient deaths at a single clinic in Kansas from fentanyl overdoses, thanks to Actiq lollipops.

Drug reps did not know explicitly how dangerous fentanyl was. But we should have known, given the lollipops. Doctors should have known, too. Instead, we—and I mean the entire medical profession, doctors, nurses, drug reps, everybody—focused not on the danger of opioids but on their effectiveness. They worked. They dulled pain. People who had trouble with daily functions were able to function with much less pain, at least for a while. People who couldn't get out of bed were back to working full days and leading vigorous lives. For a while. People were able to pick up their kids and grandkids again. For a while. Then many of them became addicted, many forever, until the end of their lives. Uncounted numbers of people overdosed, and we know that death totals climbed over two decades to more than 50,000 annually.

Many physicians were skeptical and careful, of course. But many were not. Some came to be in the pockets of the drug companies promoting opioids, rewarded richly to endorse Actiq. But most doctors who prescribed opioids, whether cautiously or enthusiastically, did so solely to help their patients, to ease their pain, to give them back their quality of life.

But some physicians went too far in response to their patients' reports that the opioids helped and pleas for stronger doses. Some doctors signed stacks of prewritten prescription forms or had forms copied with prescriptions and their signatures. Then those doctors told their nurses or assistants to simply fill in the names of patients complaining of pain. It was so routine that those nurses and assistants, dealing with preprinted, presigned prescriptions, thought that opioids must be super-safe.

The assistants became more and more likely to hand out prescriptions without a patient even seeing a doctor. And why not? Opioids were a miracle drug, in theory anyway, remarkably effective for almost everybody in pain. Little thought was given for those who might be adversely affected. Some doctors eventually came to recognize that some of their patients were becoming overreliant on opioids. No one wanted to use the word "addiction," but that's what it was.

For a patient who felt good on opioids and terrible without opioids, the only thought was to get opioids. Some doctors tried to wean their patients from opioids, and patients found their way to other doctors who would write new prescriptions. Patients began signing up with several different doctors or clinics and shopping around for new doctors who did not know their drug history and were willing to write new prescriptions. We sales reps called it "traveling on lists": patients would make the rounds of their doctors and clinics, collect opioid prescriptions, and then fill the prescriptions at different pharmacies in order to avoid drawing attention as heavy users.

Actiq was the tip of the iceberg of the opioid epidemic that soon came to kill more Americans every year than automobile accidents. This dangerous, addictive drug, designed for breakthrough cancer pain, was being widely, nearly indiscriminately prescribed for mere headaches and other aches and pains that in the past might have been treated with aspirin. A lot of those patients might have been educated to find ways to live with their headaches. But they couldn't find a way to live without their regular fixes once they were addicted to fentanyl.

I am convinced that Cephalon's embrace of off-label sales with those three drugs can be blamed on Frank Baldino's long-standing disdain for government safety regulations in general and the FDA in particular. With Gabitril, Provigil, and Actiq, Cephalon not only embraced off-label sales but also made off-label sales the company's primary path toward generating sales growth, increasing profits, and boosting the company's share price.

Encouragement for off-label sales was no longer surreptitious; sales reps were being instructed to sell off-label. Off-label sales of Gabitril, Provigil, and Actiq became part of the company's formal training for sales reps, both newcomers and old-timers like me. For a time, I put a happy face on my disapproval. I went to luncheons and dinners where doctors were paid by Cephalon to be "consultants" and gave glowing reports on one or more of the three drugs—and where doctors coached by Cephalon sat in the audience and waited for the right moment to ask loaded questions that were designed to give the speaker an opportunity to say something else positive about selling that particular drug off-label. It was staged to seem as if the endorsements were impromptu and in response to random questions, but nothing was impromptu or random.

I didn't like it. I wanted no part of the new training and no part of off-label marketing. I wanted no part of the rigged and fake programs and audiences salted with biased questions at lunches and dinners for doctors. I wanted no part of the rah-rah internal training sessions where Cephalon executives instructed sales reps on how to sell off-label effectively—and illegally. From telling us that off-label marketing was illegal and we should not do it to openly training us to do it, Cephalon began justifying off-label marketing as legal. But our trainers still told us to keep it quiet and not to admit to anyone that we were promoting the company's drugs off-label. Sales reps were confused. Off-label marketing was OK, but we couldn't admit to it? The company was lying to us, but most reps were willing to overlook the inconsistencies, especially when their commission checks came in.

This wasn't what I thought a reputable pharmaceutical company should be doing, and it wasn't what I thought honest sales reps should be doing. I tried to keep my reps in the Midwest from doing off-label sales. My people listened to me politely and sometimes argued, again politely, that if the company was not only recommending but also offering instructions for off-label sales, then off-label sales must be safe. The company wouldn't do anything dangerous, anything that would hurt patients. Cephalon trainers warned that if the sales reps didn't follow their training and do off-label sales, they would make less money— both for themselves and for the company. And if they made less money for the company—if they didn't hit their ever-increasing sales quotas as off-label marketing raised the bar—the company would demote them or maybe fire them. That was a concern of mine, too. I was willing to make less money, but I really didn't want to be demoted or fired. That's who I was: a damn good sales rep and a damn good area manager.

Ten

Demoted

*C*ephalon was becoming a different company—drinking, affairs, cheating on expense accounts. I wondered whether the coarser culture could be blamed on the message from the top: off-label sales were OK, and the rules were for other people, not us. Or were these people I worked with now more willing to bend and break the FDA's rules because they had looser morals and ethics in the first place? Did off-label marketing cause the debauchery? Or vice versa? Were people who drank too much and cheated on their spouses and expense accounts more willing to mislead doctors and put patients at risk just so they could make a little more money? Or were the company's official break-the-rules policies and training a green light to break the rules in other parts of work and life, too? I do know that as Cephalon's sales grew, many more reps were hired—and every new hire I met had absolutely no problems with off-label sales.

Throughout 2001 and 2002, gradually, mostly quietly, I let it be known—but only to a couple of executives, my bosses—that I was uneasy about off-label sales. As an area manager, I tried again to talk to the sales reps on my team about the ethics and legalities of promoting our products off-label. "That's not us," I told them. "That's not our way of doing things." But it was the rest of the company's way of doing things. Legalities didn't matter. Ethics didn't matter. What mattered to Cephalon—and to the sales reps out there peddling its products—were sales and commissions. The company began making off-label marketing part of the hiring process. It became a standard question for people applying for sales rep jobs with Cephalon: "Hey, are you OK with off-label sales?" I was becoming a dinosaur, the old guy with the outdated ethics.

If I had thrown myself into off-label marketing, I am convinced that I would still have been one of the company's most productive sales reps. But I couldn't do it. When almost every other rep in the company was putting up the best sales numbers of their lives thanks to off-label marketing, my own numbers continued to lag. My sales, always among the top 10 in the company, were suddenly not merely average but mediocre. I was no longer seen as an effective leader, as a good area manager.

I didn't object when the company suggested that I give up being an area manager and become a regular sales rep again. The company said I could stay on as a regular sales rep, one of the rank and file, but I was no longer in charge of an area sales team and no longer on the fast track to becoming an executive. I didn't argue. It was a demotion, sure, but it made sense to me, and I embraced it.

Moving down the food chain was a relief in some ways. I had not been able to convince anyone else that off-label sales were wrong, but maybe stepping out of a leadership role would let me just keep my head down and conduct my business my way, ethically and legally, without off-label sales. Maybe, I thought, my years of service and continued but limited productivity would help me keep the job as a regular sales rep.

But it was hard to accept that my dreams were dashed—I would never move up to become one of Cephalon's top executives. I couldn't provide the off-label leadership that the company wanted from me or that my sales reps wanted from me. The question became whether I would continue working at Cephalon at all. I didn't know whether I would be fired as a sales rep or whether I would feel I had no choice but to quit.

In late 2002, I began writing down my thoughts in a journal—just a small ring-bound notebook, like administrative assistants or students use for notetaking—and found that it made me feel better. It relaxed me, somehow, to express my feelings in that tangible way. I wasn't talking to anyone, and no one was listening to me, but it made me feel better. It also helped clarify my thinking and crystallize my feelings. The more I wrote about what I saw and heard and the more I reflected on how I felt about what Cephalon was doing, the more I was convinced that it wasn't right.

I was really afraid that a patient taking an off-label drug I had recommended to a doctor would cause that patient harm.

As the year 2002 neared an end, I was having trouble keeping my head down. I was especially troubled after the FDA sent Cephalon a warning letter. On the face of it, the letter reminded the company of the rules against off-label marketing. Between the lines, the FDA was telling Cephalon that the government knew what it was doing and would crack down unless it stopped. I couldn't stand by and watch the company descend into off-label sales at the cost of so much risk and damage to patients and to the future of the company itself. I went again to my immediate boss to make my case more forcefully. He didn't want to hear anything about off-label sales. It's what the company is telling us to do, he said. It's fine. Get back to work. "If you have a problem with what we're doing," my boss advised, "go to human resources."

Human resources? What would HR do? They didn't have anything to do with company sales policy. The only reason I would go to HR would be to find an exit strategy from the company, to see whether the company would give me some sort of package. Was my boss telling me to think about an exit strategy? Was he saying it was my time to leave? Eventually, it became clear that's exactly what my boss was telling me. Without saying it explicitly, he was telling me that perhaps my time at the company was up. It just took me awhile to realize it.

Then I went to John, my longtime friend in the company, who was a couple of notches above my boss in the company hierarchy, to tell him my thoughts. Our conversation was totally off the record, just two old friends talking, not company business. John readily agreed with me; off-label sales were dangerous, and the company was careening down a path that could be destructive for many sales reps and for the company itself. What we were doing was probably illegal and almost certainly unethical. "What can we do?" I asked.

"I don't know, but I'm not going to do anything more myself," John replied. It turned out that he had complained to his higher-ups, too. He had been to the company's lawyers. And he had been to human resources. They all told him to forget it—off-label sales were OK. That said it was pretty clear that if he kept pushing the issue, he was going to suffer. His career would suffer the way mine was suffering. He might be forced out. John had some health issues and needed the company medical insurance. He couldn't afford to be kicked out on his own without health insurance, especially with retirement a few years away. He told me that despite his personal misgivings, he wasn't going to raise any more red flags or complain to anyone, officially or unofficially. He had washed his hands of off-label. He was going to look the other way and keep his mouth shut. It was a matter of survival, literally.

After talking to John, I was even more frustrated and unhappy. I didn't know where to turn. I began to seriously contemplate the concept of becoming a whistleblower and going outside of the company. That Christmas of 2002, I was down in Key West on vacation, by myself for much of the time, and I thought about it a lot. But I didn't know exactly what I was doing or how to go about becoming a whistleblower. Whom should I contact? It didn't seem like something an ordinary lawyer, our family lawyer, would know anything about. I had no idea how to go about getting in touch with the Food and Drug Administration or even whether that was where to start. What could I do? Call the switchboard and say I wanted to be a whistleblower? Could I go to an investigative reporter? I wasn't even using the term "whistleblower" at that point. I knew vaguely what a whistleblower was. The guy who exposed the Pentagon Papers and the government's Vietnam secrets, Daniel Ellsberg, he was a whistleblower. Erin Brockovich, who exposed a company's pollution practices that made lots of people sick, she was a whistleblower. Pointing out that your company is selling pharmaceuticals off-label didn't seem like it was in the same league. It was hard to imagine a reporter writing a story about Cephalon selling off-label. It wasn't exactly Watergate or the Pentagon Papers. And even if it was, I had no idea how to reach out to the press. Would I just call the newspaper or the local TV channel?

And what was I going to say? Was I going to expose my friends and colleagues, the men and women I had worked with as sales reps? Would they lose their jobs? Would they be arrested? Go to prison?

While in Key West, I got a call from Sue, a registered nurse at a sleep center back home in Dublin, Ohio. We had come to know each other well not only because her office was just across town from the house where I had lived for 20 years but also because we respected each other's professionalism. I used to see her a lot when I called on sleep centers frequently, and we had gotten along.

In fact, her office was one of my favorite places to stop. She and everyone else there were polite, friendly, and, most of all, very professional. They understood my job and appreciated that I supplied them with samples that could help their patients, especially the Provigil they prescribed for narcolepsy. I had helped guide some of her doctors at the sleep center toward consulting and speaking roles. Some of them had become thought leaders in the study and treatment of sleep disorders. It was good for the sleep center, good for the doctors, and good for Sue. We had a great professional relationship, almost to the point of being friends. On the phone that day, Sue quickly wished me well and asked about the family. Then she got right to the point. She was calling to give me some news and to complain.

The complaint was that I had not been around to see her in a while. I had not dropped off any free samples of Provigil, which I used to do quite often. She and her doctors, and especially their patients, had appreciated the free samples, and now they missed them. I told Sue I was sorry. I told her I knew that her doctors liked the recognition and status that came with being thought leaders. I told her I recognized how valuable it was for the office to have ample supplies of free samples if Provigil; patients loved free samples and loved medical practices that reliably gave them samples and held down their prescription costs. However, I told Sue, Cephalon had told me and every other sales rep to stop calling on sleep centers and to stop offering free samples of Provigil to sleep centers. Sleep centers already knew what a great drug Provigil was and how effective it was in treating narcolepsy.

"Sleep centers are already sold on Provigil," Cephalon told us sales reps. "You don't need to call on them anymore and tell them about it. You don't need to sample them. They're going to prescribe Provigil anyway, whether you call on them or not." Instead, I explained to Sue, the company told us to concentrate on promoting Provigil off-label to psychiatrists, not for narcolepsy but rather to augment the treatment of depression.

That led directly to the second point of Sue's phone call: the bit of news. She had seen a story in the *Wall Street Journal* noting that Cephalon's off-label sales had been skyrocketing and boosting the company's stock price. The story also quoted Frank Baldino as saying he didn't understand how or why Cephalon was racking up so many off-label sales. To him, it didn't make sense; doctors must be figuring out the alternative uses of these drugs on their own. But he welcomed the increase in sales. Sue said his comments were aimed at investors who read the *Journal*, hoping to encourage them to invest even more in Cephalon shares—and further drive up the share price and further fatten his own stock holdings along the way.

Sue said Frank was lying; he knew exactly why Cephalon was having such big off-label sales: it was because the company was pushing its salespeople to market its drugs off-label—including promoting Provigil for depressed patients with EDS (Excessive Daytime Sleepiness). "But that's not right," Sue said. "That's not what Provigil is for. You guys should not be selling this drug off-label—or any other drug, for that matter."

I told Sue I agreed with her but I wasn't sure what to do about it. I had made up my mind to look for a new job—I had been working on my résumé while down in Florida—and as soon as I got a new job, I was going to leave Cephalon. In the meantime, I was willing to tell the FDA what I knew. But I didn't know how to go about it.

"I think I do," Sue said. "I know someone. I'll put you in touch."

I was surprised. Sue knew how I could become a whistleblower? I never would have guessed she was plugged in like that. I went through the rest of the holidays working on my résumé and thinking about my big decision—if I ever had to actually decide—to become a whistleblower. What would I have to do? What would it mean to the company? To my colleagues who had been selling off-label? What would it mean to me? And, perhaps most of all, would I have the nerve to go through with it even if I did get the opportunity?

A couple days after New Year's, when I was starting to get ready to go back to Ohio, Sue called me with a phone number. "Call this guy, Greg," she told me. "He might be able to help you." I later found out that Sue's sister was an FBI agent in Texas and her sister had found the contact for me.

I waited a couple of days. Then one afternoon in Key West, sitting at the Pier House Beach Bar with Janine Brown, I called the number Sue had given me. It was a Maryland number, from the area code. There was no identification, name, or affiliation on the recording asking me to leave a message. I left my name and number and said only that Sue suggested I call. The next day, I got a return call from a special agent with the FDA's Office of Criminal Investigations. The OCI, I learned, works closely on prosecutions with the federal Department of Justice and other federal law enforcement agencies such as the FBI. Here's how OCI is described on the FDA website:

"As FDA's criminal law enforcement arm, OCI protects the American public by conducting criminal investigations of illegal activities involving FDA-regulated products, arresting those responsible, and bringing them before the Department of Justice for prosecution."

Holy crap, I thought. This shit is getting real.

Greg, the agent calling me back, wanted to get together. I swallowed hard and said OK. A few days later I met Greg and another federal agent in the atrium of the Embassy Suites hotel in Columbus, Ohio. With their long hair and leather jackets and jeans, I thought they looked like they could be drug dealers out of the 1970s movie *The French Connection*. They were all business, no small talk. They wanted to know what I had. I explained that my company was promoting three prescription drugs off-label, touting them to treat medical conditions they were never intended to treat, with Actiq being the most dangerous and having the greatest addiction potential. The agents said this sounded like something the OCI should be investigating. Would I help?

"Yes," I said. "I'll help." Almost as an afterthought, I asked what I would have to do. I was kind of shocked by what they said. The first thing, they said, was to get together in a couple of days so I could sign the forms to officially become a federal informant. We did that, and I was photographed, my fingerprints were taken, and I signed the forms promising to cooperate with the government, to provide truthful information and evidence, and to testify if necessary. By signing, I promised that the information I provided to the FDA's Office of Criminal Investigations would be truthful to the best of my ability and knowledge. If I lied about anything, there would be penalties, including prison time. I could still be prosecuted if I was involved in any new, additional crimes committed while I was an informant. If I committed some technical violation of the law, such as not reporting others when I saw them breaking the law, I could be charged myself.

Eleven

Wearing the Wire

I began cooperating with Greg and the other OCI investigators, informing on my company and my colleagues and the doctors we called on. I gave them more background on the two drugs that I had sold off-label, Provigil and Gabitril, and how they were positioned in front of doctors for off-label prescriptions. I also told them about Actiq, the third drug in Cephalon's unholy trinity of illegal off-label drug promotions. Actiq—fentanyl, the powerful opioid—was known in the medical community; it was not understood yet in law enforcement for its problems in addiction and overdose. At that point, in the early 2000s, nobody was predicting the opioid wave that was going to sweep across the country and ruin so many lives in the coming years.

I talked to the investigators extensively on the phone, especially the lead investigator, Greg, whom I came to regard as my main handler. I met him and other agents face-to-face occasionally, usually in Columbus, a much bigger city than Dublin, where we were far less likely to be noticed together. I tried to make an effort a few times to check and see whether anyone was following me, but I didn't seem to be very good at it. I never spotted anyone, and Greg told me not to worry about it. "Nobody is going to follow you to us," he said. He made it sound like I wasn't worth following, which deflated my images of being a modern James Bond. When I told my kids about that, they laughed so hard. It's still a favorite family story.

Greg and I talked a lot, over and over, about how Cephalon recruited doctors—"co-opted" might be a better word for it—to talk about their off-label drugs to other doctors. Doctors as speakers or authors, in front of audiences of doctors or in professional publications aimed at doctors, could be tremendously effective in spreading the word and persuading other physicians to try Cephalon's off-label drugs. Many of the in-person meetings were arranged as professional medical education, organized and sponsored and paid for by Cephalon, including the topics to be covered and the doctors to address them. The nice free dinner with an open bar and unlimited good wine at a good steakhouse was one of Cephalon's favorite ways to stage an evening of CME, continuing medical education. Every doctor has to attend a certain number of CME hours per year, as required by the state where the doctor is licensed. Doctors who don't meet their CME obligations can be suspended by their state medical licensing boards. Some bigger pharmaceutical companies will occasionally reward their favorite doctors—the physicians who prescribe high volumes of their drugs or do the most to promote those drugs to other doctors through writing or speaking—with sweet paydays for speaking, such as at major medical conferences.

But the steak dinner was Cephalon's go-to move. At one of our typical steak dinners, local doctors would be invited for CME credit. One or two colleagues they respected would stand up and talk. They'd describe, for example, how Provigil was supposed to be prescribed to treat narcolepsy but it was actually an even better drug for augmenting the treatment of depression and daytime sleepiness. They'd also talk about how Gabitril was an anticonvulsant drug for treating epilepsy but was actually an even better drug for treating anxiety and neuropathic pain. Actiq was discussed in CMEs as "ER on a stick" for migraine patients. It was effective for many patients with breakthrough pain.

I want to emphasize that most CME doctor events were totally above board at most pharmaceutical companies. They happened all the time. Nothing seemed dirty or crooked or shady about these events—unless off-label sales were the underlying reason for it all. These dinners, popular across the industry, brought together doctors talking shop with other doctors, comparing notes, and offering suggestions for how to do their jobs more productively and treat their patients more effectively. The whole aura of the workshops, seminars, and continuing medical education was cloaked in the warm reassurance that this was the best way to practice medicine and care for patients. It seemed natural for drug companies to pay favorite physicians consulting fees to come and say what the sponsoring company wanted them to say in order to boost the company's sales and profits.

When I described Cephalon's steak dinners, ostensibly for continuing medical education, I know that to the investigators the whole concept of CME seemed like a blatant conflict of interest: doctors exchanging their professional opinions for a little bit of status and a very little bit of money. But to most of the doctors and sales reps at Cephalon's steak dinners—all but me, I guess—it seemed natural and made sense. These doctors offering the advice were giving up their time for the greater good of the practice of medicine. It seemed impossible that any doctor's professional opinion could be swayed by a drug company or one of its sales reps. That was unfathomable. And why shouldn't a doctor be compensated in some small way for giving up some of his or her time for the greater good? The only wrinkle in Cephalon's efforts was that push for off-label marketing. That was the problem, ethically and legally.

The Office of Criminal Investigations agents were patient and thorough to the point of being repetitive. They often asked me the same questions over and over. I came to recognize that it was part of the process of building a reliable, solid case. They needed to understand everything. And I needed to be consistent. I couldn't say something and then contradict myself the next day or the next week. I couldn't say anything confusing or that added confusion to something I had said earlier.

They never offered specifics, but the agents indicated that their goal was to build a criminal case and bring charges against Cephalon. There could be a trial if the company refused to make a deal, but more likely Cephalon would settle the case by paying a fine to avoid trial. The company might pay tens of millions of dollars, but Cephalon would be able to survive and keep selling drugs—though not off-label. That would have to be part of the settlement: no more off-label marketing.

The agents said there was a chance of prison time for one or more executives, but that was unusual and unlikely. Typically, paying a big fine would take prison time out of the equation. If the company refused to settle out of court and pay the big fine, or agreed to the fine but didn't pay it, or continued to break the law, the Justice Department could reopen the case and seek a trial for the CEO and other top executives. I knew that if and when there was a criminal trial, I would probably have to testify in open court. The agents didn't like to talk about that. I think they were afraid of scaring me off. That was fine with me; I didn't want to talk about it, either. I didn't want to testify in open court. The agents also didn't like to talk about the possibility that Cephalon would escape any charges at all. That might have frightened me more than the prospect of testifying in open court. What if I had become an informant for nothing? Cephalon certainly wouldn't want to employ me anymore. Would any pharmaceutical company want to employ me?

Greg said I was giving them good stuff and being a good informant. But he and the other investigators weren't the people

I had to convince. I had to convince the Justice Department lawyers who were in the background, reading over my statements and the agents' reports and offering suggestions for lines of questioning. It would be up to the Justice Department to decide whether there would be a case. At one point, after I had been talking to the agents two or three times a week for several weeks, Greg told me that he was confident we could build a case that could lead to Cephalon being fined by the government. He said the unseen lawyers who were looking over his shoulder agreed. But we needed more to actually move against Cephalon if we were going to put a dent in Cephalon's operation, if we were going to shut down the off-label marketing at Cephalon and send a message to doctors and other pharmaceutical companies. We needed better, more direct proof. Instead of my background information and eventually my testimony, if it came to that, they needed a smoking gun. Lots of smoking guns, actually. They needed Cephalon executives plotting the company's off-label sales strategy. They needed training sessions where sales reps were taught to sell off-label.

Greg made all that clear in several conversations that I realize now were softening me up for the big pitch, the big question. He made it after going through the evidence we had, the soft spots in our evidence, and the need for smoking guns.

"Bruce," he said. "We want you to wear a wire. Will you wear a wire?"

I had anticipated the request and thought about it. I had asked the kids about it, too. The family agreed with me: it was the right thing to do, to see this whole venture through. So when Greg asked, I simply said, "Sure."

People often ask me whether, at this point, I wish I had decided differently. I have thought a lot about that. What if I had declined to wear the wire? Would my life be better now? What would have happened with Cephalon? What would have happened to patients taking off-label drugs, especially fentanyl? Of course, I thought about all that a lot in the ensuing years.

The cards were on the table. I picked them up. I was going to play the hand of an undercover informant wearing a wire, whatever happened and wherever that took me. That's how I found myself in a resort outside Las Vegas in February 2003, getting wired up and hearing federal agents repeatedly tell me, "Speak to the collar."

After that first day of wearing a wire and speaking to my collar—and having a lot of other people speak to my collar, too—I returned to my room thinking, "This is great. There is enough here to convict the company and a bunch of the bosses, starting from the top down. We're done. We just hit a home run."

I slept well that night.

So it was demoralizing, to put it mildly, to learn the next morning that none of those incriminating statements had been recorded. They were gone, into the ether. The agent from the Office of Criminal Investigations who had wired me up couldn't understand what had gone wrong. We had to start over. I was thrown instantly into a foul mood. How could I be so stupid? I knew I had to make the best of this. I hadn't been dealt the best hand, but I had to make the best of it.

The same thing, it's hard to believe, happened the second day I wore the wire. I worked my ass off all day getting people to talk to my collar about how they would get insurance companies to pay for off-label prescriptions. The representatives would tell the staff of the doctor's office to reclassify the patient's diagnosis, ICD9 codes, International Classification modification to describe diagnosis. Reps would have staff change the codes to get previously rejected off-label prescriptions covered and paid for by insurance. And then when I got back to the agents' room, there was nothing on the recording. I was beyond angry. I was resigned when they told me we would try again the next day, after wasting the first two days of the conference.

The agents told me that they had figured out it was a faulty mic to blame, and they had a new one shipped in for the next day. It worked, finally, thank goodness. The rest of the week went smoothly. Each evening, back in my room, the agents and I talked about some of the great stuff I had captured on the tapes that day, really incriminating comments by the Cephalon bosses. At one point in a meeting in front of a room full of sales reps, one of the company's executives in charge of medical liaisons—relationships with doctors—got into a heated exchange about off-label sales with an even higher-ranking executive, a marketing guy who was one of Frank's top lieutenants.

The medical director was complaining that the programs he set up to educate doctors were being hijacked and misused by the company to build momentum for off-label sales. That was wrong, he said. It was unethical and maybe illegal. The medical director specifically mentioned a doctor who had complained that he had been hired to help run one of Cephalon's continuing education programs for doctors, and he was being instructed by the company to say things he didn't believe in order to promote off-label sales. The doctor said that Cephalon was crossing the line for what was legal and ethical.

"No," the Cephalon marketing executive fired back. "He has no right to tell us where the line is. We hired him. We will tell him where the line is." At the same meeting, another high-ranking Cephalon marketing executive boasted that it had been her idea—not any doctor's idea—to promote Provigil and Actiq off-label. A few sales reps expressed unease about misrepresenting drugs and selling them for treatments without any medical assurance that they would work, or at least not cause harm, but the marketing executives reassured them that study results were coming. The studies would come in a few weeks and confirm that the drugs being sold off-label actually were safe and effective. Once those study results were in, the drugs would be sold on-label, as they were supposed to be. They wouldn't be off-label anymore, and no one would have any complaints about legalities or ethics or any of those other minor concerns.

Not at that sales conference or anywhere else did we sales agents ever see any study results confirming the effectiveness of the drugs we were selling off-label. We never saw any study results on those drugs at all. The company just wanted us to keep selling, selling, selling. That was the unrelenting message. Screw the rules and keep selling off-label. All this stuff captured on tapes—the company executives incriminating themselves and Frank Baldino—was gold for the investigation. I also got a lot of good recordings—good for the government, bad for those particular sales reps—of colleagues over dinner and drinks in the evenings. I didn't participate much for or against off-label marketing in those discussions. People knew how I felt, but I don't think anyone had the faintest suspicion that I was wearing a wire and they were giving potential evidence. I mostly listened as other sales reps echoed the views that most Cephalon agents were expressing. Some had no qualms about off-label sales; the company told them it was OK, so it must be OK. A few had some misgivings about off-label sales but tended to take the company's word for it being safe and acceptable and not risky to anyone. If there was a problem, those reps reasoned, the company would cover for them. And besides, everyone agreed, they loved the additional money they were bringing home every month thanks to off-label sales.

After the debacle of the first two days, I wore a wire again for the remaining three days of the conference with no problems. It was at least eight hours each day, at every meeting, at every cocktail hour conversation, at every informal, supposedly private conversation with another Cephalon employee. Each evening I would return to my hotel room, and Greg and two other OCI agents were waiting for me. They carefully removed the wire and debriefed me. That didn't take long because they basically wanted to know whether I had any problems during the day. I hadn't. They didn't need to hear from me about what I got on the recordings that day; they would listen to the recordings themselves, and so would other people. Each evening, they reminded me to get in conversations about off-label marketing and how the company encouraged it but not to seem like I was forcing the topic. They were especially interested in the workshops that two executives, a sales vice president and a lead trainer, were running to highlight off-label marketing techniques.

Most evenings I couldn't go right to bed. I made notes in my journal, which was still kind of a new thing for me. Mostly, I made notes recalling conversations I had with people, whether or not my wire had been working. But sometimes I made comments on my role in the whole undercover operation. Interestingly, at that point I was trying to protect the company. I was afraid that off-label marketing was going to sink the company and I would be out of work. My priority was not to sink Cephalon; my priority was to sink the bad bosses, end the bad off-label marketing, and restore the company's ethics—and ensure my job would continue. "I know I am on the right track," I wrote one night, "and this is the only direction to take to try and save the company and my job."

Twelve

The National Sales Meeting Busted

*O*n Friday, the last day of the sales conference, the meetings were scheduled to end midafternoon, then there would be some free time before a cocktail hour and a closing dinner. Most people were flying back to their respective homes the following morning, though a few had made arrangements to stay for the weekend and play golf or move to a proper gambling casino-hotel on the Las Vegas Strip. I suspected there would be some wild partying for some of those folks. Nobody invited me to stay around.

After the last formal business meeting of the conference on Friday afternoon, I went back to the agents' room to get unwired. The agents had just opened the safe in their room and pulled out three shiny gold badges and three shiny black handguns.

I was surprised. What were they going to do? Were they going to arrest someone? Whom? Were they gonna pull their guns to make the arrest? They ignored my questions, as usual—"What, are you guys going cowboy now?"—but Greg finally turned to me.

"You need to go take a walk now, Bruce," he said.

"What?" I truly did not understand. A walk? Where? Why?

"Yeah," he said. "Get out of the hotel. Now. Stay out at least an hour, hour and a half." I walked out of the room a little dazed, with three agents clipping badges onto their belts and strapping guns in holsters over their shoulders. I heard them mention something about a manager and a trainer, but I didn't hear any names.

Down in the lobby, I approached the front door. I had no idea where to go. This was not a popular hotel in a popular spot. After all, it did not have a casino. It was sort of out in the desert, on the edge of town, not even close enough for an easy walk to a casino. No bars nearby, not even a coffee shop. At least it was February, and it wasn't blazing hot the way it would have been in the summer or even in the spring. But I was going out for a walk—government orders—so I stepped toward the door. Suddenly, one of the young reps from one of the Southern states stepped in front of me. "Hey, Bruce," he said. "Where you goin'?"

I was taken aback—was he spying on me for the company?—but quickly reminded myself that as a senior sales representative and one of the company's top-selling reps, lots of younger hires looked for opportunities to talk to me. Some probably thought

I might be their boss someday. Others may have figured I could offer some tips on how to sell more or how to negotiate the company politics and advance their careers. There was a time that might have been true, but not anymore. "Hey, man," I replied, forcing a big grin. "I'm on my way for a walk, a little exercise and fresh air. I don't know about you, but I've been breathing hotel air all week."

"Cool," the young guy said. "That sounds good, actually. Is it OK if I go with you?"

"Sure," I said, doing my best to shrug nonchalantly. "Come along."

The two of us took a nice leisurely stroll down the semidesolate road that would eventually have taken us to the airport. There was a sidewalk, but we didn't see anyone else walking as we covered maybe a half mile, until we found ourselves on the edge of the desert and the sidewalk disappeared. Then we turned around and walked back exactly the way we had come.

The young Southern sales rep was a nice kid. He probably would have had a promising future with most drug companies. But I didn't feel like I could offer much encouragement or assurances right then, not with the trouble Cephalon was getting into. I didn't say anything about off-label sales, even when the young guy brought it up. I didn't think he was fishing for comments from me; I didn't think anyone sent him in the hopes of getting me to admit I would be willing to talk to the FDA about what Cephalon was doing to promote off-label sales. It seemed like he simply wanted to talk. It wasn't widely known at that point that

I objected to off-label promotions. Only my bosses knew that. But everybody was talking about off-label. The young guy asked me about the FDA and off-label sales, though. He wondered what might happen. What did I think? I didn't know, I said. Whatever was going to happen no doubt depended on what was going down behind us at the hotel and who was being confronted by three agents with badges and guns. But I didn't say anything to him about that and tried not to think about it myself. Anything could happen, I told him.

He pressed me. Did I think the FDA might bring charges? I had no idea. What could happen to him if Cephalon went down? Again, I had no idea. He was really afraid of losing his job. He had gotten married the previous year, shortly after starting at Cephalon. He had been doing well at the company, and he and his wife had recently purchased a new house. They had extended themselves with the mortgage—overextended themselves, actually, since they were relying on his sales commissions continuing to rise over the next few years, just as they had risen in the past year thanks largely to off-label sales. The young guy said that if he lost his job, that might mean losing his house, even if he got another job right away. And his new bride would not be happy about that.

Tired and thirsty, we walked back into the controlled climate of the hotel lobby. The blast of icy air felt clean somehow, but I still wanted a shower. The young guy said thanks, shook my hand, and headed off to his room. Just as he left, turning the corner from the lobby into the hall with the bank of elevators, around that corner into the lobby came Frank Baldino. He greeted me with the same easy style I had seen many times.

"Hey, Bruce," he said. "What's up?"

"Hey, Frank," I replied, nodding to the bar across the lobby. "I'm just gonna get a drink."

"Great," he said. "I need one, too. I'll join you."

This little meeting was noticed by every one of the Cephalon sales reps and executives and trainers in the lobby, probably two dozen or more men and women. They watched intently as Frank and I, as casually as a couple of golf buddies, strolled up to the big wooden bar and slid onto a couple of stools, side by side.

I could all but hear the wheels turning and the murmured questions: What's going on? Why is Frank having a drink with Bruce? I was intensely aware that all eyes were on us, but Frank seemed totally unconcerned. We started talking about the conference, what I had liked, what he had liked, what we could do differently and better at the next sales conference. I don't know whether he had heard about my objections to off-label marketing. If he had, he didn't show it. It didn't seem like he was sounding me out or probing for any hints or waiting for me to give it away that I was an informant.

The mood in the bar was upbeat. Several groups of Cephalon employees were in the bar pregaming for the evening's festivities, just as Frank and I were doing. I'm sure those other Cephalon folks, like Frank and I, were going over the highlights of the conference, comparing notes, doing a little happy post-conference work. Those other Cephalon employees could look over at us and see the CEO, relaxed and smiling, happily chatting away. Those other Cephalon employees had to be feeling good. It had been a good conference, with lots of information and inspiration on how they could conduct their business even more efficiently and profitably.

That happy mood was about to disappear.

Thirteen

My Cover Blown

*A*s Frank and I chatted in the hotel bar, I realized that bedlam was breaking loose behind us in the lobby. Cephalon employees—sales reps and managers and top executives, more of them flooding into the lobby by the minute—were gathering in groups of two or three or four, all talking excitedly. They were coming into the bar and breaking into groups of coworkers who had been relaxing over their drinks. I heard a couple of people saying, "Did you hear what happened? What happened? The Feds? The FBI? Who were they after? Somebody was arrested?" I wondered what Greg and the other agents had done.

First one, then another, then a third executive came up to Frank as we were taking the first sips of our drinks. More executives, and a couple of the same ones, approached us again.

"Uh, Frank, excuse me; we need to talk to you."

"Frank, we've got something of a situation. We need you upstairs, please."

Each time, Frank waved them off. "C'mon guys, it'll wait. I'm having a drink with Bruce."

I think he suspected that his lieutenants just wanted to get him away from me; it was not good optics for the boss to be seen with the guy who had misgivings about the company's embrace of off-label marketing, let alone a guy who had recently been busted down from area manager to sales rep. But in the bar, Frank was feeling good and motioned toward the other Cephalon folks in the bar, including the ones trying to talk to him and pull him away.

"Bruce," Frank instructed, "buy a round for all our people in the bar."

This was a significant signal. The handful of managers and executives senior to me raised their eyebrows at this; they were the ones who should have been buying a round for the bar, not me, a guy who was clearly on a downward career spiral. Laughing inside at their discomfort, I reminded myself that Frank had known me for a long time and probably still considered me a senior guy, too. I was one of his early managers, and the two of us had always been cordial, even friendly. Then two vice presidents—sales and marketing—came up to Frank and insisted that there was a true emergency and he needed to be informed. Upstairs. In private. "We have a problem," one of them said ominously. Frank took a last sip of his drink, cool as a cucumber, stood up, shook hands with me, and told me we'd sit down together again soon for another drink.

"That'll never happen," I thought. I was right.

As far as I know, only Frank and a small circle of his executives left the hotel that weekend knowing what had actually happened upstairs. I didn't find out until the following week, when I was back home in Ohio talking on the phone to Greg, whom I had come to think of as "my" federal agent. He told me that after the last presentation of the conference had concluded—it had been breakout sessions for different regions on how to best ramp up off-label marketing in their territories—Greg and the other two agents had come into the meeting room where my team was meeting. A manager and a trainer had been instructing us sales reps on the fine art of getting away with off-label marketing. They were the last two people I recorded at the conference. I had split as soon as that breakout session was over, heading to the agents' room to be debrief and unwired—and told to take a walk. The agents never told me they were targeting the leaders of the session I had just been in. All they told me was to take a walk, and I did. Now, days later, I was hearing from the agents what had happened after that.

As the manager and trainer were gathering up their materials and talking about how it went, Greg and the other two federal agents came in, showed their badges, sat the two Cephalon employees down, and told them that they had evidence that the company was breaking the law by inappropriately promoting Provigil and Gabitril off-label. The agents apparently never mentioned an informant or anyone wearing a wire. They suggested that they wanted the manager and trainer to work with them—to flip—to avoid criminal prosecution by answering their questions and giving them evidence.

The two Cephalon agents seemed shocked, Greg indicated to me, but neither seemed especially surprised to be confronted by federal investigators looking at Cephalon's off-label sales. To the agents' dismay, the manager and trainer both said no. They said they would not talk to the agents without their lawyers present. This put the agents in an awkward position. They could have arrested the two Cephalon employees and tried to question them later, with their lawyers present. Arresting them was out of the question; the agents did not have a particularly strong case against either of them. And the Department of Justice was not especially interested in prosecuting these two. They were small fish, and convicting them would not bring the kind of fines—in the tens of millions—the government had in mind. The feds wanted to prosecute Frank Baldino and other top executives and force Cephalon to pay hundreds of millions in fines.

Neither Cephalon employee confronted by the federal agents said anything to them at first and not much to them later during their brief encounter—probably not more than 10 minutes. Frustrated, the agents handed the two Cephalon employees their Department of Justice business cards and said, "Get in touch if you reconsider and want to talk to us." Then they let them go.

The agents' goal had been to use the confrontation as a way to elicit more information—information that I didn't have and didn't come up in my recordings. When they "badged" the Cephalon employees—that is apparently cop talk for that sort of confrontation—the Office of Criminal Investigations agents were looking for higher, better sources than I was. The agents had been hoping for a quiet flip: that one or both of the employees would agree to provide evidence and maybe Frank and the rest of the company would never know until actual criminal charges and lawsuits were filed. But the agents' hope went out the window when the Cephalon executives refused to cooperate. The agents had been hoping that mere intimidation and the fear of going to prison would have led one or both Cephalon employees to cave in—to agree, on the spot, to turn government witnesses, to provide evidence in the hope of getting a lesser charge or avoiding charges altogether.

When the area manager and trainer fled the conference room and their confrontation with Greg and the other federal agents, they went looking for the highest-ranking Cephalon executives they could find. They wanted to tell Frank what had happened and let the company know that the Justice Department was coming after Cephalon. No doubt they would have told him everything, but he was down in the hotel bar having a drink with me. They told some other executives, who told some other executives, and they all asked each other where Frank was until they figured it out and headed for the bar, excited as hell. I could see the panic and anguish and urgency on their faces—and I knew why—as they tried to extricate Frank from our casual barstool conversation. In a way, it was funny, the way he put them off for a few minutes until they were too insistent to ignore and he shook hands with me and followed them out of the bar and up to someone's room for a debriefing and powwow.

Meanwhile, I was besieged in the bar by Cephalon employees. Bruce, what's going on? Bruce, did you hear about the raid? Bruce, what did Frank say? Bruce, is it true that the FBI arrested some of our people? Bruce, are they gonna arrest us, too? Bruce, Bruce, Bruce . . .

No, I told them, Frank didn't say anything about whatever is happening in the hotel. No, I didn't know anything about what was happening in the hotel. No, I hadn't heard anything about arrests. Or the FDA. Or the FBI. Or a mole in the company. No, I had no idea whether Cephalon was going to be shut down. No, I didn't have any more idea than they did. Funny enough, not one sales rep asked me why the company might be in trouble or what the government was investigating.

I think everybody knew it was the off-label marketing. They knew, just as well as I did, that what we had been doing was illegal. The young rep who had gone for a walk with me earlier came up at the predinner cocktail party, really worried. He had heard that the FBI had tried to arrest some Cephalon people. He wondered whether there was a chance he was going to be arrested. That would be the end of his marriage. He really didn't want to go to prison just for doing his job the way he had been trained to do it.

I listened sympathetically and resisted the temptation to tell him—and several other sales reps who expressed similar concerns to me about the FBI being in the hotel—that it wasn't the FBI. I could have told them: the FBI isn't the investigative arm of the Food and Drug Administration; the FDA has its own set of investigators, the Office of Criminal Investigations. The OCI investigators have the same investigative authority and the same power to arrest people as the FBI, but OCI is a different law enforcement agency, specializing in things like off-label sales. No, I didn't reveal any of that to the Southern sales rep or anyone else who asked me later. I didn't want anyone wondering how I had come to know so much about the FDA's criminal investigations.

I'm a pretty easy guy to read. My emotions are never far from the surface, and I rarely am able to hide them. I think I'm a better salesman for that same reason; you see what you are getting, and it doesn't look like I am hiding anything. But somehow for that half hour or so in the bar, I was positively sphinxlike: unknowing, unspeaking, giving nothing away. Sorry, guys, I don't know anything. No, Frank didn't say anything to me about the FBI.

I asked my anxious colleagues what they knew or what they had heard. Turns out they didn't know much but had heard a lot, much of it untrue, like that the agents were FBI. Again, I didn't bother to correct them. When one of them asked me whether it was true that someone—one of us—had been wearing a wire throughout the conference, I looked as innocent as I could and said, "Wow, really?"

Besides, I didn't know much more than my colleagues. I may have known less. I hadn't heard anything beyond what they were telling me at that moment—and what Greg and the other two federal agents had told me in their room before they sent me out on a walk. And they had not told me much. I had no idea whom they targeted and tried to turn, or what they had said, or whether they had made any arrests. After half an hour or so of questions from them and nonanswers from me, I took leave of my colleagues in the bar and headed to my room to check my phone and email and finally get the shower that had been delayed when Frank grabbed me as I came back into the lobby from my walk. The shower helped, but it didn't relax me as much as I had hoped. I was still on the tightrope, very publicly, when I came back downstairs for the conference-ending cocktail hour and dinner. Officially, it was still business as usual at the conference. Except it wasn't business as usual that evening.

Everyone at the cocktail hour was still buzzing about what had happened, or what they had heard had happened, or what they thought had happened. I still knew next to nothing. There had been no messages for me from Greg. I resisted calling his room, figuring he'd reach out when he was ready to tell me something. I had learned that early in the informant game: I didn't ask questions. They asked questions, and I gave answers. By the time we gathered for the cocktail hour, I wasn't getting the same level of questioning. It might have been because so many people had tried to talk to me earlier and figured out that I didn't know much.

Uncharacteristically, Frank was not livin' large at the conference-ending cocktail party. He was not the life of the party as usual. He didn't come to the reception or to the dinner. I heard that he had flown home in his private jet as soon as he got word about the agents badging the two Cephalon employees.

At the cocktail party, Baldino's right-hand men were smiling, laughing, shaking hands, rubbing shoulders, slapping backs, as if everything were normal. I could sense a mix of relief and reassurance filtering through the Cephalon crowd. Maybe there was nothing to worry about after all. When one of Baldino's top lieutenants spoke, it became immediately clear that he had scrapped the usual uplifting rah-rah speech he or Frank usually gave to conclude these gatherings of Cephalon executives, trainers, and sales reps, a couple hundred people in all. This time the Cephalon executive didn't deny or deflect anything about FDA investigators being at the conference, nor did he explain much. But he made it clear that the FDA was coming after Cephalon and that the company was going to fight back against the federal government.

"Well," he began, "the sons of bitches busted us." Then he launched into the most profane public speech I have ever heard, one cuss word after another, often in creative combinations. He said we reps had not been doing anything wrong. "You're doing everything right," he said. It was the government agency that set the rules that was wrong, he promised.

"We're going to fight this," he stormed. "And we're going to win." By the time the Cephalon executive wrapped it up, most of the audience was cheering and clapping. They may have felt differently in the cold, sober light of morning, but for that brief time on that evening, everybody seemed to think Cephalon was indeed going to beat the US government. When he came off the podium, I was the first person to shake the executive's hand. I wanted to make sure everyone saw it.

He grasped my hand and held it a little too long, looking me right in the eye. "Bruce," he asked meaningfully, "are you all right? Are you really OK?" I sputtered, Yeah, sure, I'm great. But I was thinking, He knows that I wore a wire, and I am a dead man in this company.

But nothing happened, at least for a while. Home in Ohio after the sales meeting, back at work, I was hoping that rubbing shoulders with the brass—the drinks with the CEO earlier that evening, that long handshake with the top lieutenant after his fiery speech—would help defray suspicion of me as the mole. In fact, I was more of a suspect than ever. Remember how the federal agents had given the two Cephalon employees their Justice Department business cards and told them to call if they changed their minds? Well, one of the Cephalon employees tossed the card aside while leaving that meeting room where they had been questioned. The agents didn't find the tossed-aside card before they packed up and left. But Cephalon executives, revisiting the scene, did find the card. The card was from the Justice Department's Office of Criminal Investigations in Columbus, Ohio.

Why Columbus? Why was the Justice Department using agents from Ohio? The agents pounced in Nevada. Why not agents from Las Vegas? Cephalon was based in Pennsylvania. Why not agents from Philadelphia? The FDA was based in

Washington, DC. Why not agents from Washington? The Cephalon executives didn't need to be geniuses to figure out and to draw a straight line to Bruce Boise, one of two Cephalon sales reps based in Columbus, Ohio, and the only one in the whole company who had been moaning and groaning for months about the direction the company was headed with its off-label marketing.

Before long, everybody in the company seemed to know about the business card. And here's a funny thing: No one said anything to me about it. Nobody asked me how those agents from Ohio got the notion to investigate a company that was based in Pennsylvania and had offices all over the country. Nobody asked me whether I knew the agents. Nobody asked me whether I was the informant. But it was pretty obvious that everybody was convinced I was the bad guy.

I felt it in the way they spoke to me in person or on the phone, in the careful restraint in emails, in how they looked away from me in one-on-one conversations. More and more people avoided contact with me of any sort. People looked at me differently, strangely, weirdly. I wasn't the guy they thought I was. I was a threat, a real danger to them and to the careers and lifestyles they had worked so hard to build. I could take it all away from them.

Fourteen

My Dismissal

*A*fter that conference in Nevada, through the spring of 2003, Cephalon people I had trained and promoted and people I had been friends with met with me in person only if they had to, like at an area sales meeting or one of the company's steak dinners or other events for doctors—which I was still attending, as if nothing were wrong. Those people who had been my work friends tried not to get caught in a conversation with me or sit near me. They refused to look me in the eye and exchanged only the most perfunctory greetings—hi, howya doin'?—and then the turn away to talk to someone else, or concentrate on the speaker, or go get a drink, or just study their phones. Anything but talk to or be seen talking to Bruce Boise. For a gregarious guy like me, for someone who had felt so close professionally to these folks, that was difficult. But there was nothing I could do about it. I was their kryptonite.

Not long after that explosive conference in Nevada, Greg told me that Cephalon had hired a big-name law firm to defend against any coming charges and find out what it could about the OCI investigation. The law firm, Greg told me, had "done business" with the FDA in the past and knew how these investigations worked and how to maneuver so its clients could get the best deal: no criminal charges, no one going to prison, and an out-of-court settlement that the company could live with. Lawyers from the law firm began making their way through the company, interviewing employees, looking for the whistleblower, and trying to figure out what kind of incriminating evidence the FDA might have gathered. "Trying to limit our exposure" is the way one Cephalon lawyer put it. I was one of the first interviewed, but not the first. That would have been too obvious, I suppose. The company probably wanted me to think I wasn't suspect No. 1. Fat chance of that. I knew there was a target on my forehead. But not coming to me first gave me the opportunity to gather some gossip from around the company on what Cephalon was asking people. I got asked all the usual, innocuous questions, but I was asked several questions that no one else was asked.

"What is your definition of off-label?"

"Are you working with the FDA?"

"Are you part of an FDA investigation?"

I stayed as nonchalant as I could and acted like I was just as curious as everyone else about what the FDA was doing, whom the informant might be, and what kind of trouble the company might be in. There was no lie detector. Nobody was put under oath. The questioning took a few minutes and seemed pretty standard. The lawyer who had questioned me seemed like he was irritated with me, maybe even angry at times. He especially didn't like it that I could quote chapter and verse from the FDA regulations when he asked me, "So what do you think is wrong with off-label marketing?" It wasn't what I thought that was important, I told him; it was what the FDA regulations say.

And then there was a lull before the storm for a few weeks. I just kept doing my job as a sales rep, no longer an area manager, a fallen star, still making a decent living by the standards of most American working stiffs but barely half the more than $300,000 a year I had been pulling in. That's because I still refused to sell off-label. Another company sales conference was scheduled for June, but it was a regional conference, in Cleveland, and wouldn't have all the brass and all the pomp and circumstance of the national meeting the previous February outside of Las Vegas. I told Greg about it and said I was going. It was part of my job to go, and it would have been weird if I didn't. Greg wanted me to wear a wire again. "The tape we got already is really good," he said. "But we'd like some more, just to make sure."

No, I said. We had enough. I could wear a wire again, to another company gathering, another sales conference, an evening event at a steakhouse, and it wouldn't make much difference. I wouldn't get a lot of stuff that was better or more detailed or more incriminating than I had gotten already. Besides, I said,

"They suspect me. They are going to be watching me. They are going to be looking for me to be wearing a wire. They are going to try to catch me, and if I wear a wire again, they probably will. I'm not going to do it."

To my mild surprise, he and the other agents did not argue. I think they agreed: I had done enough, and the risk of getting caught was much higher. I wasn't sure what the company or any other sales reps might try to do to me, but I imagined dire consequences if I was caught red-handed wearing a wire. If some guy thought my exposure of the company's off-label promotion might cost him his job, why wouldn't he, in the heat of anger, try to hurt me? If Frank thought I might bring his company down and send him to jail . . . well, I didn't want to consider the possibilities.

At that sales reps' conference in June, to my surprise, the sales managers told us again, despite the high-profile off-label investigation, that neither Cephalon nor its employees were doing anything wrong. In effect, Cephalon was doubling down and thumbing its nose at the FDA and the Justice Department. The message at the conference: We are not backing down. Screw the government interference. Screw the government regulations. Screw the government.

One sales manager said it was not up to us, to the company, to decide what was legal and what wasn't in terms of off-label sales. That manager said that off-label sales had been part of the pharmaceutical industry forever and that many other companies successfully ran off-label sales campaigns. "But one rep in our company clearly doesn't think we should be in the off-label business at all." And then he mockingly recited the very words I had uttered to the Cephalon lawyer who had interviewed me.

Everybody laughed, as if that notion was ridiculous, that it was ridiculous to think there could be anything wrong with off-label promotions. I knew that manager was talking about me, and he knew it, and at least some of the other Cephalon executives in the room knew it. But most of the sales reps laughing did not know that Bruce Boise was the informant, the guy trying to take their hard-earned money out of their pockets and the food off their tables. Even though they did not know that I was the informant, I realized at that moment that I had to leave Cephalon as soon as possible. But I didn't want to simply walk away. I wanted to see whether I could get a package. I figured Cephalon was probably willing to pay me to go away. Turns out I didn't have to do much more to make all that happen.

After that meeting, back in Ohio, I was given an improvement plan by my immediate boss. It was an impossible plan, probably illegal for all that was being asked of me. The plan was nine pages of things I had to do—not off-label sales, though. My goals included 21 action points loaded with target sales figures to hit, some of them figures I had never hit in my best years—nor had anyone else. That improvement plan was very clearly the company's invitation for me to leave. I took it to HR to see what they thought and to ask about an exit package. The HR staffer I talked to was quite familiar with my improvement plan. Clearly, it had been widely discussed in the office. She had been expecting me.

I doubt anyone had seen an improvement plan quite like this one. The HR staffer who saw me basically confirmed that and said she didn't blame me for coming in to ask about an exit package. "If they gave me an improvement plan like that," the HR person confided, "I'd leave, too."

She had the details of my exit package right there. I said I'd take it home and think about it. Five days later I accepted the package. I was pretty happy with it. I had been making about $300,000 a year, including a $130,000 base pay. The key part of the package: I would get six months' base pay, $65,000. That seemed to be fine with me. I reckoned I would coast quite nicely on $65,000 for the next few weeks. With my experience and my record both as a high-flying sales rep and as the area manager for a consistently productive sales team, I figured that my biggest problem in getting a new job would be deciding whether to be a sales rep or an area manager. I luxuriated in mulling over the choice. Sometimes I thought I'd prefer to jump back in as a manager, the person in charge. Sometimes I thought, no, I'd rather keep a low profile and be in charge of myself only. Sales rep or area manager—it was a first-world problem.

I wasn't worried about money. I had investments to fall back on if needed, but I was sure I wouldn't need those, either. I'd get a job right away. I figured most of the $65,000 severance from Cephalon would go into the bank or investments.

Fifteen

Losing Everything

*I*t soon became clear that I was not taking any long scuba-diving vacations right away. My first few months after leaving Cephalon were divided between some pretty casual job hunting and some pretty intense work with Greg and others from the Office of Criminal Investigations.

They had so many questions, new ones and old ones. I explained over and over the relationships between doctors and sales reps and the relationships between Cephalon and its sales reps. Continuing medical education, speaker programs, steak dinners, consulting fees—we went over it all, again and again. As the agents dug deeper, I added more and more, such as how some doctors allowed some sales reps to go through their patient records and offer suggestions for getting more prescriptions covered.

The investigators wanted to know chapter and verse about the doctors' roles and how continuing medical education programs were in effect being subverted by Cephalon into off-label sales propaganda. The investigators asked for more on the smallest details and the inner workings of the business, including how Cephalon and doctors regarded—and disregarded—the printed pamphlets, or package inserts, that the FDA required in every prescription, including very pointed instructions on how the drug should be used.

Many of the new questions for me from investigators came from going through the company records and statements from Cephalon. I was often asked, "What does this mean? Is that important?" I'd try to remember the circumstances and context and explain what was going on at Cephalon at the time and how it affected the company's relationship with its sales reps and then the sales reps' relationships with the doctors who were their customers. I also talked, though not as knowledgeably, about the impact of Cephalon's off-label marketing between doctors and their patients.

The Cephalon marketing department sent the sales reps lists of doctors who were HVPs (or high-volume prescribers) in certain therapeutic classes. This included, for example, pain specialists prescribing a lot of opioids; they might be interested in learning more about Actiq. Other HVP lists might focus on psychiatrists prescribing high volumes of antidepressants; they might be amenable to learning more about Provigil. Reps were required to call on their top 10 prescribing doctors at least once every four weeks. Like in so many other businesses, 80 percent of the prescriptions came from 20 percent of the doctors.

That summer and autumn of 2003, when I was newly unemployed and devoting more time to looking for a new position, the investigators introduced a new wrinkle to take up my time and attention—they had me review interviews that Greg and other investigators were conducting with Cephalon employees. From our conversations and the investigators' questions, I could tell that Greg and his colleagues regarded the case against Cephalon as anything but a slam dunk. Yet they always told me things were going great with the case. I couldn't shake my doubts. Yes, what the company was doing with off-label marketing was wrong. But could the government build a case that would prove it? And that it was dangerous? Could the government prove that the company, from the CEO on down, was knowingly and willingly conspiring to break the law that was designed to protect the public?

Relying on my years as a sales guy, I tried to read the investigators—what they said and how they said it, body language, all that. And what I saw from the investigators was that they were less than certain, no matter what they told me, about whether they were going to bring down Cephalon or even get the company to stop its off-label marketing campaigns. I had new doubts about myself. What if I had not done enough as a whistleblower?

What if the investigation did not get the proof that was needed to bring down Cephalon or at least get the company to stop selling off-label? What if the government said Cephalon hadn't done anything wrong and the company's sales reps were allowed to keep misleading doctors—and endangering patients—because the FDA couldn't prove they had broken any rules? What if Cephalon had been right all along about off-label marketing really being OK? I had to wonder: what if everything I had done—becoming a government informant, blowing the whistle, wearing a wire—was a waste? What if I had turned on my colleagues and lost my job—and maybe my career—all for nothing?

For weeks, and then months, I responded to lots of job openings, first for pharmaceutical sales reps and then for sales managers. I talked to some people, letting them know I was available and asking them about opportunities with their firms. Given my résumé—it was golden, with all those sales awards—I thought I would get lots of offers once the word got out that I was available. But that didn't happen. I had initially decided I wanted a basic, no-fuss sales rep job. I didn't want to be an area manager again. Sure, being a manager was more money but more responsibility, too. I wanted to simplify my life. I didn't have all the financial responsibilities I had when I was married and the kids were growing up. I later found out that recruiters going over my applications for sales rep jobs were suspicious: What happened to this guy? Why had he stepped down to a lesser job at Cephalon? Why, with that golden résumé, was he aiming for a sales job? When I finally figured out this was an issue, I began applying for sales manager jobs, too. If I had to take the added responsibility, I'd do it. I just needed a job—any job.

I got lots of interviews, dozens of interviews. But nobody said, Hey, come work for us. It also may have hurt that I always made it clear that I wanted to stay in Ohio. That's where I had lived and worked my whole life. That's where my kids were. I didn't want to start over somewhere else.

I wasn't worried about getting another job—until I was.

The money was going out faster than I had imagined. I was trying to maintain the same lifestyle I had when $300,000 a year was coming in. I didn't want to skimp on the kids' lifestyles or my own, but I had a lot of overhead: my own three cars, including a little sports car that I didn't drive all that often; the big house we had raised the kids in and where a couple of them still lived with me, dividing time between me and their mother; and the rental house we had purchased in Athens, Ohio, where the kids could live while they were going to Ohio University. I was surprised at how quickly my bank accounts—already diminished by the divorce settlement with Beth—drained away and then how quickly I was decimating my 401(k), which was also considerably smaller after the divorce. I began thinking about bankruptcy, but I was too proud to ever go talk to a lawyer or financial advisor about it.

I started selling stuff. The kids were upset when the cars they had been driving since they got their licenses were repossessed. They had been fully supportive of the whistleblowing thing when it didn't have much immediate impact on their lives, and I was reassuring them that I would get a new job soon and everything would be back to normal before they knew it. But now it was affecting them. Yet none of them said anything critical of me, and they were always encouraging. Less than a year after taking the package from Cephalon, I sold the two houses. I got far less than they were worth. It was late 2003, and the real estate market was heating up across the country, but I needed to make quick sales because the bank was threatening to foreclose on them. I used that money to pay off bills, but it didn't last long. It got to the point that I couldn't make my child support payments required under the divorce decree. Beth could have taken me back to court. She conceivably could have gotten me thrown into jail. But she told me to pay when I could. She knew that it was killing me not to have a job and find myself in so much financial trouble after disastrously misjudging both my job prospects and my finances. Beth's boyfriend at the time was furious with her for letting me off the hook, but she stood up to him. "Bruce would pay it if he could," she told him. "Bruce will be good for it."

As I was losing my house, I was losing my health, too. I had been suffering from a bad left hip for years and telling myself that I'd get it fixed once I got a new job and my personal situation stabilized a bit. But I wasn't stabilizing, and my hip was getting worse. I need a new hip, but hip replacement was major surgery and very expensive. I needed to get it done in the late autumn of 2003, while I was still covered for a few more weeks by the health insurance I'd had with Cephalon.

I moved in with my brother, a successful architect, and our mother, who had moved in with him. She had wanted to stay in the family home where she and my dad had raised us, but ever since he died a few years earlier, she had been rattling around in that big old house. My brother, Rex, who is single, had plenty of room for our mom with him in his three-bedroom house. It would be much better for her to live with him, my brother realized, but he had to convince her that the move was not so he could look after her but so she could look after him. My twin brother is a great guy.

When I moved in with them to recuperate after surgery, in a special hospital bed set up in the living room since I couldn't do stairs yet, my mother had me to take care of, too. She also did her best to look after my daughter Meredith, the youngest of my three kids, who was in her last year of high school and had been living with me until I sold our house.

It was a big change for all of us, this new three-generational extended family living, all jammed into a three-bedroom house that had been a comfortable bachelor pad for my brother for years. But it must have been especially difficult for Meredith, a smart, sensitive 17-year-old whose world had been turned upside down.

I was worried about her older brother and sister, too, but they were grown and out of the house. Michelle was in college, and Eric was out on his own. But for Meredith, still at home, it was a time in her young life when she needed stability and familiarity with both the people and the places in her life. Instead, she had to uproot her life from the only home she had known.

The man who had been her rock—me, her dad—was all of a sudden a crazy wild card in her life. I kept telling myself that moving in together was good for all of us. The family held together and actually got closer during our toughest times. Family, including my mother, brother, and kids, is certainly what got me through it all.

"What a huge price to pay for doing the right thing," I wrote in my journal. "Little did I know how difficult this would be on me and most of all my kids."

Those first few months after I left Cephalon showed me how badly I had miscalculated, not only about getting a job but also about having enough money to live on and keep supporting my kids. I was already dipping into investments and assets I had told myself were untouchable.

When I first told my family I was going to become an informant, my kids were fine with it. I like to think they saw me as a hero, doing the right thing. I explained that there could be repercussions. I could lose my job. Don't worry, Dad, they said, you'll get another job. The only one in my immediate family who was against it was my mother. She wanted me to forget all "that whistleblower stuff," as she called it, and just take care of my family. This wasn't any of my business, she believed, and it was not helping with taking care of the family. When I told the kids—Eric, who was then 23; Michelle, 20; and Meredith, 17—that I was going to wear a wire, that didn't seem to bother them. They thought their dad knew what he was doing. They were no doubt alarmed, at least a little, when I left Cephalon. But I had told them I might lose my job and reassured them that I could get another job, probably a better job, with no problem, whenever I wanted to. I believed it. I began wondering whether I would have to change careers and look for work outside the pharmaceutical industry. But that was really all I had ever done in my two decades of work in my adult life. I was faced with the same dilemma I had when I quit the sporting goods store. What was I qualified to do? What was I going to do with the rest of my life? I had no easy answers.

Sixteen

Who Will Represent Me?

Greg and my other government handlers, including the lawyers handling the case for the Justice Department, knew about my struggle to find work and my financial woes. They knew how much it was wearing on me. But there was nothing they could do about that to help me—or nothing they were supposed to do, anyway. I discovered that the United States has a procedure for whistleblowers to be rewarded through *qui tam* lawsuits. My son, Eric, who had taken Latin, told me that qui tam means "who brings," from an ancient English common-law concept of awarding people who brought problems to the attention of the king, especially examples of theft or deceit that were taking money out of the royal coffers. Formally, the full Latin phrase is *"qui tam pro domino rege quam pro se ipso in haw parte sequitur,"* and it refers to those who sue not only on their own behalf but on behalf of the king, too.

The more immediate American legal precedent for this law, formally known as the False Claims Act, also known as the Lincoln Law or the Informers Act, dated back to Abraham Lincoln, who pushed for the courts to set up a way to encourage citizens—and Union Army soldiers, especially—to report instances of fraud and theft.

Guns, ammunition, uniforms, food, and other supplies were being sold off on the black market before they could reach the soldiers fighting the Civil War for the North. A particular problem was defective guns; rifles that would not fire properly were being manufactured quickly, shoddily, and cheaply and sold at full price. That's where the "false claims" came from: people submitting bills to the government for contracts they didn't fulfill, for products they didn't produce, and for work they did not complete.

Lincoln wanted to stop the corruption, and he figured maybe the best way to do it was to reward everyday people who witnessed the wrongdoing. He wanted to offer financial encouragement to step forward and report the crimes. As the qui tam procedure evolved, it became part of a powerful two-pronged approach, both civil and criminal, to fighting wrongdoing. Citizens who were part of qui tam lawsuits could be awarded a share of the fines paid to the government by the wrongdoers.

Greg told me, "You need to find an attorney right away."

I was alarmed and confused. I had no idea what Greg was talking about. I needed an attorney? What was I in trouble for? I should file something? What should I file?

From his reaction, I think Greg was stunned at how much I didn't know. No, he explained, not especially patiently. Nobody had filed anything against me.

My only goal as a whistleblower was simply to get Cephalon to stop the unethical and possibly illegal off-label sales techniques. It never occurred to me that I might benefit financially from blowing the whistle. When I did some research, I discovered that as an originator, or relator, you could be awarded funds from a fine.

I was grateful to be told to get a lawyer. Greg looked out for me in major ways sometimes, like keeping my identity hidden within the agency. Even his fellow agents, when I wore a wire undercover, didn't know my true identity but only the undercover ID number assigned to me by the Office of Criminal Investigations. I would soon learn, though, that there was nothing easy about the process, starting with finding a lawyer.

I tried to meet with an assistant US attorney in Columbus to talk about qui tam law, but that government lawyer—like Greg and any other government employee—apparently was not supposed to give me much, if any, information about how it all worked. This government lawyer wouldn't even see me. My calls weren't returned, and when I went to the local federal building, the security people wouldn't even let me in. I was still in the dark.

Greg had given me the name of a private attorney in Cincinnati who apparently handled qui tam lawsuits, and I went to see him, but nothing came of that, either. He spent most of our meeting telling me what a great attorney he was. When he asked a few questions about my case, he dismissed them—and me. He didn't think I had a good qui tam case, but I found out later that the use of qui tam lawsuits was relatively new in terms of pursuing settlements from fines against pharmaceutical companies.

I found two other firms in Cincinnati that supposedly handled qui tam lawsuits. The lawyer I saw at one of those firms, harking back to the Civil War roots of the qui tam concept, told me he specialized in qui tam cases in which the false claims had been against the government, as in the case of military suppliers. The lawyers at the third firm I visited in Cincinnati seemed interested and said my case sounded promising. I was really happy about that—until they called me a week later and said they were not interested after all and wished me good luck in finding another law firm.

I was getting worried. What if more people filed qui tam lawsuits ahead of me? I hadn't become an informant for the money, but if there was money on the table, it seemed only right that I should get some of it. What if the potential rewards led someone else from Cephalon to flip and testify against the company in order to cash in? I specifically thought of the area manager and the trainer who had been "badged" and asked to become government witnesses by the agents handling my undercover operation when I wore a wire in Nevada. If one of them flipped, the Justice

Department might be a lot less interested in me, and I might become a lot less important in the pecking order for sharing a qui tam settlement if there ever was one someday.

I watched a number of movies about whistleblowers, including *The Insider*, starring Russell Crowe as the tobacco company executive who blew the whistle on the industry. He produced the secret corporate documents showing that cigarette manufacturers knew all along that their products were dangerous but they kept denying it and kept selling their product. I was intrigued with one of the true-life characters in that movie, Lowell Bergman, an investigative journalist who took up the cause of the whistleblower and helped him prove it.

"Where," I wondered in my journal, "is my Lowell Bergman?"

Frustrated, and with no one else to turn to, I resorted to googling "qui tam attorneys." Several law firms and lawyers popped up. I got on the phone to several of the firms, all around the country, in a series of cold calls that I hoped sounded professional and competent. One firm, Phillips & Cohen in Washington, DC, called me back within a couple of days. I knew nothing about the firm other than what was on the internet. One thing that was pretty clear was that the firm handled big qui tam lawsuits and that one of its star lawyers was a guy named Peter Chatfield.

By then I was feeling very uncertain. It all felt so weird because these conversations with lawyers were so unfamiliar and I did not know what I was doing. I was explaining myself and my actions, motivations, and thoughts to one person I didn't know after another. Perhaps the worst part of it was feeling that I did not know whom to trust. I wanted to trust the government people, the investigators and the lawyers, but none of them—other than the OCI agent, Greg, in a couple of big ways—had been especially helpful to me. They had been looking out for their investigation and for their court case, not for me. If I ended up as collateral damage, well, too bad for old What's-His-Number.

The handful of private lawyers I'd met hadn't inspired any trust. They didn't seem to care about me. My case wasn't easy enough. I knew the case wasn't cut-and-dried, no matter what they told me. Neither my case nor I fit into their mode of doing things. "I have made my peace with the idea that there may be no money to be got out of a False Claims Act lawsuit against Cephalon," I wrote in my journal. "I can live with that, and it was still worth doing."

After my disappointment with other lawyers and law firms, talking to the people at Phillips & Cohen gave me a little hope. The first time I talked to Peter's assistant, I simply put it out there: "I am an undercover informant for the Department of Justice helping build a case against the pharmaceutical company Cephalon."

"We're interested," the assistant responded.

In further preliminary conversations, the people at Phillips & Cohen at least seemed to be listening to me. They were indeed interested. When I finally got to talk to Peter, two or three calls into the process at Phillips & Cohen, I was even more reassured. He listened and asked questions that showed me he thought I might have a good case. He really liked it when I told him that I had been keeping a detailed journal. I had a time line laid out with what happened, when it happened, what other people were saying, and how I was feeling. Peter asked me whether I would fly to Washington to meet with him. I said sure but told him I didn't have any money for a flight from Dublin, Ohio, to DC. He said they would take care of getting me to their office.

This made me feel pretty good, in the moment. Someone was finally taking me seriously. Whether or not I would ever get any money, it felt like the case against Cephalon was going to make a difference in the world. The qui tam lawsuit could have that kind of impact, whether I collected anything or not. When I made contact with Peter, I was living with my brother in Dublin, and I told him the law firm was flying me out and renting a car for me at the airport. "A Mercedes," I told my brother. "They must think I'm pretty important." But little did I know how big a False Claims case against Cephalon could be.

Rex's reply showed one of the many reasons why he is a great brother. "Nah," he said, waving me off and laughing. "If they thought you were really important, they'd be sending a Mercedes to pick you up. With a *chauffeur*."

When I walked into Phillips & Cohen and was ushered into a conference room, I was impressed. The place oozed class. I was even more impressed when I met Peter and his colleague, Erica Kelton. I could tell that they were both among the upper echelon of lawyers in Washington, the elite of the elite. Things felt even better as we talked.

I told them the whole story: how I had been a successful sales rep, living a great life and loving my work, until I saw my bosses and my colleagues at Cephalon in effect lying and cheating—and potentially harming innocent people—all to make a little more money in commissions. I told the lawyers how I had been ostracized and shunned within my company, how I had been out of work and broke and struggling emotionally. I told them I was surprised and pleased with the possibilities of some compensation, some reward, through a qui tam lawsuit but I couldn't find any lawyers who would listen to me or take me seriously. As all this spilled out, Peter and Erika listened to me. They took me seriously. They took notes. They asked sympathetic questions. And they asked other questions, strategic questions, that I could tell were critical to building a legal case on my behalf. From all those years as a sales rep and area manager, I had developed some sort of intuition that let me be pretty good at picking up on people, their real motivations and concerns, and what they are thinking even if it is never stated explicitly. I think it's a side effect of my nonlinear, peripheral thought process, my way of thinking. And everything I thought and felt was positive about Peter and Erika and their firm, from the very beginning.

I felt such relief. I could trust these people. Maybe I was going to be all right. Maybe my life wasn't going to always be as dreadful as it had been for the past few years. At one point in that conference room, in that first face-to-face talk, I was so overcome with emotion that I started tearing up. "I'm sorry," I said, dabbing my eyes. And from them I felt nothing but sympathy.

They didn't see me as being weak or selfish. They understood my struggle, what I had been through.

Erika stood up and came around the big shiny wooden conference table and put her hand on my shoulder. "Don't worry," she said. "We're going to look into this. We'll get back to you."

The firm still had to decide whether to formally take my case. It had to go through the usual reviews that any big law firm conducts before agreeing to invest considerable money and legal brainpower on behalf of a client who could not afford to pay any money for a retainer. Sure, the firm would be getting a contingent fee, 40 percent of whatever money I was awarded in the lawsuit. If I was awarded $10 million, the firm would skim off $4 million. But I had to accept that the firm would also be making an expensive investment up front, with no guarantee that it would collect anything. It might end up with 40 percent of nothing. Its lawyers would be spending a lot of time on the case instead of on cases where clients paid the usual hundreds of dollars per billable hour. And there would be lots of administrative, travel, and other incidental expenses. I knew that by taking my case, Phillips & Cohen anticipated that I would be in line for an award in the several millions, at least. If the firm thought I was going to get "only" a million or two, it would not be interested in my case.

Phillips & Cohen formally took on my case in September 2004, filing a qui tam complaint under the False Claims Act on my behalf in the federal court for the Eastern District of Pennsylvania, the jurisdiction where Cephalon's corporate headquarters were based. "Great news about lawyers taking case," I wrote in my journal, "but still a long way to go. A lot could go wrong . . . I still think there are problems ahead and slim chances for $$$." The complaint was against Cephalon for off-label promotion of Actiq, Provigil, and Gabitril.

Peter would be my lead lawyer. My case would be folded in with the other qui tam cases filed against Cephalon. None of the other plaintiffs had been directly involved in the investigation, and none of them had provided background as an informant or gone undercover wearing a wire. But Peter said two of them had filed their lawsuits before mine and I was third in line. He said that probably meant they would get a larger share of the settlement and fines than I would. I was less concerned at that point about where I was in the line to get money than whether there would be any settlement at all.

The Justice Department still had not formally decided whether to file charges against Cephalon. The qui tam lawsuits could proceed whether or not the government brought charges, but Peter told me the odds of a settlement—and larger financial penalties against Cephalon—increased greatly if the Justice Department decided to prosecute the case.

That decision, I knew, depended largely on how good a job Greg and the other investigators did. And that would depend largely on the strength of the information I had provided.

Seventeen

The Smoking Gun, New Evidence

At one point well into the investigation, Greg had big news for me—good news, he said. The Department of Justice had made the decision to commit to prosecuting the case against Cephalon. Instead of it being strictly a Food and Drug Administration regulatory case, the US attorney in Philadelphia was interested in bringing criminal charges. This raised the stakes, Greg told me. Overnight, the investigation against Cephalon had become a much higher-profile case for the government. Eventually, I had to go to Philadelphia and talk to Marilyn May, the US attorney for the Eastern District of Pennsylvania.

I had been in Philadelphia a number of times in the recent past, always for visits to the Cephalon headquarters in the suburbs. On those visits, I had been intent on doing everything I could to support Frank and further the company's goals. Now, only a few miles away in a federal office building downtown, I was a key part of an investigation that could mean the end of Cephalon and send Frank Baldino to prison.

Marilyn, like any high-ranking federal prosecutor, was cordial but all business. She came to know me pretty well, and she sympathized with my trouble in finding a new job. But in my initial meetings with her, she was totally focused on the investigation and emphasized one big point: she needed more evidence to make the case. Without more evidence, she made clear, Cephalon might get away with it. Frank Baldino would get away with it. And she didn't say it in so many words, but if Cephalon got away scot-free, I would have thrown away my career for nothing. My background information was necessary and critical and important. So were all the recordings and transcripts we had gathered at the sales conference in Nevada. But it was literally all talk. Did I have anything written? Any memos or company directives? Even any emails? Were there any instructional videos showing Cephalon sales reps how to market the company's drugs off-label? I had turned over sales materials, emails, doctor visit notes, and more that discussed and described off-label promotions.

I told Marilyn about John, the longtime friend and Cephalon sales executive who had tried to complain about off-label promotions to the company in-house lawyers and human resources department. I told her that he had been involved in creating training materials to show Cephalon sales reps how to market off-label.

She wanted to talk to John. I told her he would say no, but she kept asking. I kept saying no. They wanted John, who was the director of the pain division, in charge of promoting Actiq. They wanted to interview him. Next best thing, I would talk to him.

They said they just wanted to find out what information he had and what evidence we didn't have yet. In the back of my mind I thought perhaps John would welcome a chance to help with the FDA investigation. After all, he had been the one other person in the company, besides me, who seemed to have real problems with Cephalon's off-label marketing. The investigators told me John's evidence or testimony could be the nail in the coffin that ended off-label sales not only at Cephalon but at other companies, too. His testimony could mean that thousands of patients all over the county would not suffer needlessly because they had been given the wrong prescription drugs.

I had left the company a year earlier, but I still had not been identified by Cephalon as the informant. I didn't know whether John would take the call, but he did. John seemed happy to talk to me about Cephalon's off-label marketing and about his role in it.

Right there, on the call, John laid out why he would not flip. He would not become a government witness. He was afraid he would lose his health benefits. He was so afraid of this happening that he went on short-term disability in anticipation of retiring. His thinking was that it would be harder for the company to fire him or otherwise punish him if he were on disability. He told me over the phone that he would not be interviewed in person by the investigators. And he certainly would never testify in court.

However—and it was a very big however—John told me about a PowerPoint presentation Cephalon had put together to train sales reps in the basics of off-label promotions. It laid out, step by step, the company's instructions to sales reps: *Here's what you can say to a doctor. Here's what not to say. Don't promise anything. Let doctors decide. Tell them only what the product does, including side effects. Don't talk about conditions or diseases being treated or cured. Talk only about symptoms and how some other doctors are trying these other off-label drugs for some of those symptoms.*

The PowerPoint was explicit—and creative—in some of its advice to Cephalon sales reps. It targeted physicians we sales reps had no business calling on, including doctors who didn't ordinarily prescribe the drugs we marketed. Our drugs were not on-label; package inserts for the drugs did not include treating the medical conditions that those doctors were treating. Sales reps could give those physicians free samples of anything they asked for. Thanks to the First Amendment, Cephalon assured its sales reps, they had a constitutional right to market off-label and to leave those brochures anywhere they wanted, including in a doctor's office.

Who was the FDA to overrule the US Constitution? John sent a copy of the PowerPoint to me, and I passed it along to Marilyn and the FDA investigators. Along with all the incriminating tapes I had gathered in Nevada, it did indeed nail down the case. The PowerPoint showed not only that Cephalon talked about off-label marketing but also that the company taught, trained, and coached its sales reps to sell off-label. This was the smoking gun that the prosecutors had been looking for.

After our initial conversation, John and I talked many more times during the investigation, both on the phone and in person. John was nervous about being seen with me, so we met in coffee shops where neither of us were known and were unlikely to run into anyone who knew either of us. He still seemed nervous. He told me that Cephalon executives had issued a blanket edict: nobody in the company should talk to Bruce Boise. Even if they didn't have proof that I was the informant, I was still their No. 1 suspect.

After John and I had been talking for a few weeks, into 2005, he told me he had spoken to a few other sales reps at Cephalon who had expressed misgivings about off-label marketing. He told me he had indicated to them, carefully, without mentioning my name, that he might know of ways they could talk to the government investigators in secret. Two or three dozen sales reps—I was surprised it was so many—said they were interested or at least would consider it. Some backed out. John said one of those sales reps with qualms had apparently secretly taped conversations with her sales manager about how to market Cephalon products off-label. He never identified that sales rep, and she never came forward. Several times I called sales reps who had spoken to John about their discomfort with the company's off-label marketing. The first thing some of them said was "Hey, I am not supposed to be talking to you." The second thing was "Goodbye."

Every conversation John or I had with sales reps was confidential. These were sales reps we had known for years;

they trusted us more than they trusted the company. I passed everything along to the OCI investigators but without ever identifying individual sales reps. Most of their information was background, but good background.

One sales rep outed himself in a very twenty-first-century way. He handed me his company laptop. "The feds can have whatever they want from it," he told me. I told Greg about it, and he arranged to get the laptop from me and for the laptop's contents to be scoured by OCI's technical people. There was a lot of good stuff on the laptop, Greg told me, but nothing new. Everything had already been collected from other Cephalon employees. He gave me back the laptop, and I gave it back to the sales rep, who seemed disappointed.

The OCI agents never reached out to him. He, like a growing number of Cephalon sales reps, had come to see the company as mistreating them and potentially betraying them. It was becoming increasingly clear that the company was training them to do something illegal and possibly positioning them to take the fall if there was a criminal crackdown. More than one Cephalon sales rep, contacting me privately, asked, "Bruce, am I going to prison over this?"

John told me that Cephalon had also told its employees not to help me with my job hunt. They were not supposed to say anything about me, good or bad, to anyone outside the company. They were not supposed to provide references to potential employers, either positive or negative, for Bruce Boise. I knew that Cephalon was, in effect, blackballing me in the pharmaceutical industry, but it was good to have that confirmation, to know one big reason my job search was going nowhere. When I started looking, in those first few weeks after my departure from Cephalon, I concentrated on sales jobs; I thought it would be easier for me to get a lower-level sales job than to aim higher. After what I'd been through at Cephalon, I didn't want to be anybody's boss. I wanted to just go make my own sales, stay in my lane, keep my head down—at least for a while. Maybe I'd get back on the fast track at some point, but I wanted to make sure the timing was right. Besides, there were a lot more open positions for sales reps than for area managers. With that recalibration, I reckoned I was sure to get a job quickly.

But that didn't happen. After a few months, I started wondering why I wasn't getting a job. I wasn't even getting many interviews. Part of it, I told myself, was that I was an older guy, in my fifties. Even with my experience, I didn't have as much upside, in terms of how long I could contribute to the company, as somebody 20 years younger and cheaper to hire. I began to realize it was suspicious that I was out of a job that long. I imagined what other drug companies were saying about an application from Bruce Boise, who not long ago had been a heavy hitter in the business. What could be wrong with this guy? So successful, then he leaves his company suddenly? Why?

I suspect that when any prospective employers were willing to give me the benefit of the doubt and check me out, all it took was one quick phone call or email to someone at Cephalon who would say, "Oh, yes, Bruce Boise. Can't talk about him."

I suspected that if requests for information about Bruce Boise went far enough up the Cephalon chain of command, some of the top executives might be authorized to offer a quiet word about me. "Oh, yes, Bruce Boise. Sad case. Went off the deep end. We think maybe he was a government informant, passing along all sorts of stuff that wasn't true about our off-label sales, which are fine. You know Bruce got divorced recently, right? He's had a lot of trouble."

I don't know for certain whether there were conversations like that. But I imagined. I was toxic not just at Cephalon but also across the pharmaceutical industry.

I was getting even more discouraged with the job search. Being an ex-Cephalon rep did not feel good. I found that Cephalon's reputation in the pharmaceutical industry was suffering from its off-label marketing campaigns. Other companies thought Frank was cheating by breaking the rules and didn't like it when their sales reps noted that Cephalon's sales reps were making lots more money because they were allowed to go off-label.

Then I got a call from an international biotech firm with a good reputation and offices in Ohio. Over the course of several interviews with several different executives at the biotech firm, I was asked repeatedly about Cephalon's off-label sales. At first, I thought the biotech firm was asking for more information so they could avoid the pitfalls of off-label sales themselves. But then I began to suspect that they wanted to know more about how Cephalon was organizing its sales force to go aggressive on off-label sales so they could copy Cephalon's methods and have their sales force go off-label, too.

It was no secret that a number of other pharmaceutical companies were also envious of Cephalon's dramatic increase in revenue thanks to off-label sales numbers. I thought the biotech firm wanted to cash in, too. I answered all the interview questions, but eventually it became clear to the interviewers that I was not a fan of off-label promotions. And I was not interested in teaching the biotech firm's sales reps how to be better off-label sales representatives. Eventually, I stopped hearing from the biotech firm.

After not hearing anything for weeks, I got a call from the same firm. One of the managers was interested in me. He said he was going to hire me and set the process in motion. He even booked travel and hotel for me at the company's upcoming sales conference in Chicago. I was happy and relieved. My life could get back on track.

I came into the company headquarters for what I thought was going to be one last round of introductions to the few top executives I had not yet met. I had just gotten a relaxed conversation going with the guy who was hiring me when we were interrupted. He was called out of his office. He stepped out, and a few minutes later a security guy came in and asked me to follow him. He led me to the door. I was being escorted out. It was humiliating.

I asked around with some of the people still talking to me at Cephalon, and they indicated that executives at Cephalon—who had agreed in my separation agreement not to give me a bad reference with possible future employers—had warned the biotech firm against hiring me. There was nothing I could do about it because there was no way for me to prove that actually happened. I imagine the executive who had invited me back ended up getting chewed out pretty good for trying to hire me.

In all, I applied to several dozen jobs, for both sales rep and area manager. It took me awhile, but I eventually realized that I was being hurt by more than just my age and my connections with Cephalon. I was hurting myself. I was submitting good, positive applications. When I was called in, I was not interviewing well. I wasn't myself. I was uncertain. I had no confidence, no self-assurance. In a tough moment of self-awareness, I realized I was never going to get another job in the pharmaceutical industry. It was difficult for me to wear two hats at the same time: undercover informant for the government and someone still following the company line. I was so disillusioned by Big Pharma's corruption.

During our otherwise all-business conversations, the US attorney, Marilyn, sometimes asked me how the job hunting was going. On one of those occasions I mentioned the debacle with the biotech firm. I told her that the firm apparently had been interested in me only for background and coaching on how to conduct off-label marketing. She was really interested in that. Was the biotech firm doing off-label marketing, too? I told her I didn't know. Let's find out, she suggested. No, I said, I am hoping my days of wearing a wire are behind me. Besides, I didn't think the biotech firm would ever allow me on the premises again, and it seemed pretty clear that none of the biotech executives would get into any sort of conversation with me, especially a conversation that might incriminate them over illegal off-label sales.

As we got deeper into the investigation, my handler, Greg, made an offhand comment that intrigued me. He said I had shown a flair for investigative work; I understood what it meant to gather evidence and build a case. He said that if I was looking for a job, and especially a new career, I might consider becoming a federal investigator. "Bruce, you're good at this," he said.

I was flattered, of course. And I felt like I really had been good at it—keeping a journal, wearing a wire, providing the necessary background for the investigators to make their case. I idly wondered: Could I change careers? I was looking for work, after all. But a federal investigator? It seemed unlikely. I was good at sales. Little did I know, though, how difficult it was going to be to find work in my field—or in any field, for that matter—ever again.

Eighteen

Blackballed from the Industry

I did not do well with handling the transition out of Cephalon and eventually, slowly, painfully out of the pharmaceutical industry. I had been a professional man, a success. Now I was not only without a profession but also without any sort of job at all. And I was near homeless, if not for the grace and generosity of my brother, Rex, who let me live with him. He let my younger daughter, Meredith, live with us, too, long enough to finish high school.

"I have no way of paying my taxes," I wrote in my journal. "I will have to sell all, and I'll have very little." I had tried everything to get a job. I had tried pharmaceuticals, wound care, cardio implants, and even hospital sales for supplies—so many résumés and applications and interviews for jobs outside of Big Pharma.

I tried real estate, home siding sales, retail sales, insurance sales, car sales, and so much more.

During my six weeks of recovering from hip surgery over the winter of 2004–2005, I didn't do any job hunting. By the time I got back on my feet, I had little desire to go through that fresh hell all over again: looking online for openings, calling and re-calling everyone I knew in the industry for cold leads, tweaking my résumé for each individual application, writing and rewriting and polishing each cover letter, sending out the letters, and then . . . nothing. Waiting. And more nothing. I didn't want to do it anymore. I had come to the cruel, hard fact that I was probably never going to work in the pharmaceutical industry again.

When I was demoted from area manager, I had accepted that my dreams of becoming a top drug company executive were never going to be realized. Now, somehow, it was hard to accept that I'd never be a drug rep again. No more sales calls on doctors. No more serious clinical discussions about neurology with some of the smartest neurologists in the country. Never again an area manager overseeing and managing and coaching other drug reps. No more sales conferences. No more president's inner circle platinum awards for selling so many doctors on writing so many prescriptions. I had no future at all in the pharmaceutical industry.

I withdrew during that time. I probably became depressed. When I was strong enough, I began walking gingerly around the neighborhood: first just a few feet from the condo, then a little farther and a little farther. Slowly, my hip began feeling like a part of me, and I got stronger. Poking around my brother's garage, I found an old six-speed trail bike. The tires were fat and flat, but I pumped them up and went for a little spin. I hadn't been on a bicycle in decades, but I could still ride a bike. It's true—you never forget. That old bike became my main mode of transportation. I rode it year-round, including through the ice and snow in the winter, for four and a half years.

I struggled emotionally, waiting to hear what was going to happen with the case against Cephalon and how to find a way to feel like a productive, competent person again—and to make enough money to put food on the table for myself and, I hoped, provide some of the financial help my children needed as they were launching their adult lives.

Not everyone was sympathetic. I remember one winter day when I was riding my old bicycle to Kinko's to use a computer and make some copies. I did that a lot, since I didn't have any office equipment anymore—and it was a treacherous trip because of the ice and snow. I was afraid I was going to fall and break my new hip. A car pulled up next to me at a stop sign, and the driver put down the window to talk to me. It was a guy I had known a long time, my mother's accountant, who also served as her stockbroker and her financial adviser. He said hello and asked how I was doing, then grimaced and said, "You really lost it when Beth left, didn't you?"

That was so upsetting—to distill and dismiss everything that had happened to me into one glibly cruel comment—that I wanted to get off the bike and hurl it into the side of his car. But I needed a working bike; I simply didn't say anything, and he drove off.

After my hip surgery, when I finally mustered the energy to start applying for jobs again, I tried to stay in health care even if it wasn't going to be in pharmaceutical sales. I was a salesperson, after all, and I should have been able to sell anything. I got a job with a company that offered wound care products to urgent care clinics. I hated it, and I didn't last long. The same with my brief stint working for a company that sold cardio implants, including pacemakers and stents. These weren't bad jobs; they just weren't for me. My heart wasn't in them. Neither was my mind. I was grieving for the life and career I once had.

I felt like I was imposing too much on Rex, so I moved out and began staying with friends. One friend let me move into his partly furnished basement, which apparently had been his dog's territory until I arrived. I would often come back to find that the dog had peed on the couple of suitcases that I used to carry my scant belongings from place to place. Perhaps pathetically, I still carried neurology journals around with me. I'd come home from another day of failure and sit down with them at night to read about the science and the work that had once been so important to me.

I moved five times during one 12-month period.

"I have been down so long," I wrote in my journal, "I am not sure how I would act if I got a break right now."

I tried real estate. I tried selling home siding for Sears. I was hired by a home construction company to sell houses on spec.

None of that stuck. I began picking up work here and there painting houses and found that I liked the simplicity and clarity of that kind of manual labor.

Eric, my son, and I started a painting company together, first one job then another until we became known for our good work. But I blew out both shoulders, and that career was over before it got started. I wrote a lot in my journal at night, too, and that seemed to make me feel better. It offered some perspective, even if I was ending entries with notes such as, "All is lost."

A friend arranged for me to see a counselor, and after resisting—I didn't need a shrink—I found that talking to someone really was therapeutic. I realized that I was struggling with a classic case of clinical depression. But it didn't take many sessions for me to begin turning things around. If I ever find myself even starting to feel depressed again, I won't hesitate to find a psychologist or psychiatrist to counsel me. It helped me manage the hardships I was facing.

Another thing that helped me was a steadier gig. It was manual work, too, but I enjoyed it: manning the food stand that my friends Dave and Becky took to fairs and festivals throughout Ohio. In the morning I helped set up the tent in the park, playground, or parking lot or along the main street. I chopped onions, I flipped burgers, I took orders, I made change, and I found myself smiling back at people as they told me how they liked their bratwurst. I loved the carnival business. Work was simple—and hard. Festivals were fun and a happy time. As my dad used to say, "All work is honorable."

Dave and Becky paid me $10 an hour, but that job was huge for me. I would return to wherever I was crashing after a 10-hour day at the food stand, with the crisp new $100 bill Becky had given me in my pocket, bone tired, the smell of fried onions in my hair, and my clothes stained with ketchup and mustard. And I would feel good about the day and what I had done. It was reinvigorating for me.

I gradually realized there was something to be said for not owning anything. No big house, no big cars, no investments. Rather than always wishing for things I didn't have, I began to look at life differently. I came to appreciate the little pleasures and to be happy for the small victories I got out of life. My natural positive attitude was reenergized. Life was good.

Once the Justice Department got involved in the case against Cephalon, I had to spend even more time on it. At times it seemed as if I was being asked to dredge my memory for everything I had ever learned not only about the company but also about the pharmaceutical industry in general: everything I had learned, everything I had seen, everything I had heard—everything. It was tedious at times and exhausting, but it was also a welcome distraction from my personal life.

As the federal investigation into Cephalon continued, I kept waiting for the company to change its policies and to scale back on the off-label marketing. I didn't expect the company to admit to any wrongdoing, but I expected that Frank would try to limit the company's exposure and his own personal liability. Frank would never admit he was wrong, but I thought he would try to reach some sort of mushy-language compromise with the government. Maybe the company would say that, yes, it technically broke the rules under the arcane interpretations of the FDA, but the rules were vague, and, besides, nobody was hurt, and many people were actually helped. Frank would admit only to being ahead of his time; it was tough to be a genius sometimes.

But that didn't happen. From the moment the FDA tried to flip those Cephalon employees at the Nevada sales conference where I wore a wire, the company doubled down on its commitment to off-label marketing. Instead of changing its way and easing back on the off-label marketing in order to avoid culpability and reduce any potential fine, Cephalon refused to admit that it was doing anything wrong or to scale back the off-label marketing. I was surprised at this, but Greg, my main handler, shrugged. He said it made sense, I wrote in my journal. "If they change, they are admitting guilt." And Frank Baldino and Cephalon were going to admit nothing. They were going to fight.

Before long, 90 percent of Cephalon's Provigil sales were not for its indicated treatment, for treating narcolepsy, but rather for off-label treatments for fatigue, depression, hyperactivity, attention deficit disorder, and drowsiness caused by other prescription medications. It was also commonly prescribed as a drug that made you smarter, that literally made your brain work better. Not only were military pilots taking it, but thousands of college kids pulling all-nighters were, too.

In the early stages of the FDA investigation, through 2003, if any Cephalon sales reps asked about whether they would get in trouble with the government for off-label marketing, the company simply told them not to worry because the FDA wasn't going to do anything. Indeed, Cephalon seemed to be doing everything it could to increase off-label sales. Frank Baldino continued to show complete disdain for the FDA and a complete commitment to off-label marketing. Taking their cues from the top, the sales managers told their reps, "Let's keep doing what we are doing until the company tells us it is wrong." Then and now, it's hard to find a lot of fault with the sales reps for selling off-label. They were doing what they were being trained and instructed to do.

My friend John, still at the company, still waiting to be eligible for his retirement, told me that when some of Cephalon's ⸰ top sales and marketing people had quiet conversations with the company lawyers, the lawyers reassured them, No need to worry, the FDA didn't have a leg to stand on. John told me that at the next national sales conference, in 2004, marketing executives told the sales managers that the FDA couldn't do anything to Cephalon. "They can't touch us." He told me about a sales conference where the company had actors come on stage, acting like patients with pain issues, begging for off-label prescriptions of Actiq. The actors, after begging for prescriptions of Actiq for their pain, then testified on stage to the Cephalon sales reps— acting the whole time, reciting from scripts the company had provided them—about how effective Actiq was and how much it helped them live with less pain. It was pretty hokey, John said, but it had sales reps cheering and all fired up to go out and do some off-label marketing of Actiq.

Through those years, I had many ups and downs over the case. In the absence of a real job, gathering evidence for the investigation sort of became my job. Just as I would be feeling good when I had a good day at work in the old days, I would feel better if Greg reported something positive to me about the case. If he didn't call me back—which happened a lot—or if he had less than positive news, I tried to stay up. "Even if there is no money or fee involved in this," I wrote in my journal, "it has been one hell of a ride." I had numerous entries like that.

Here's a typical sequence from my journal: "I have this feeling that things will work out. It's that ridiculous optimism that I have. I know I am watched over and it will always work out."

And then a mere four days later: "I was very down today. Too much owed in taxes, no job and no plans . . . It seems the future is dim."

Nineteen

The Relators Standoff
and a Move to Florida

*B*y early 2006, Cephalon had grown to more than 3,000 employees, and a leading industry trade publication named it one of the 10 most respected biotechnology companies in the world. But not long after that, later in 2006, came what I regard as the pivotal point in the case. Cephalon was sending up to 11 lawyers at a time to meetings with Marilyn May in an attempt to dissuade her from filing criminal charges and to try to get her to drop the case. It's my understanding that a key meeting came when a group of Cephalon lawyers flat-out challenged Marilyn on what the investigation had found and whether she had any smoking gun, anything to really prove that the company was officially promoting off-label marketing.

The US attorney up to that point had been keeping her cards close to the chest. As far as I know, despite all the rumors and suspicions about me, Cephalon and its lawyers still did not know for certain whether I had been wired at that Nevada sales meeting or anywhere else. I suspect that they thought they would have known sooner if the government had any particularly damning evidence. They didn't know what was on my recordings, and they did not know that the government had the PowerPoint presentations that John had given me, the one in which company trainers in effect told salespeople how to do off-label marketing.

The government also had added a relator that used to be a pain care representative selling Actiq. He had very specific evidence of wrongdoing by Cephalon and its off-label marketing of fentanyl. In his territory he had doctors writing for unapproved uses of Actiq, including names, dates, and company instructions.

Then came that meeting where the Cephalon lawyers again challenged Marilyn to show her cards or back off on the criminal charges. She had been waiting until the case was strong enough, and at that moment it finally was. She showed them some of the evidence and played one of my recordings, one that was with a Cephalon vice president boasting about how it was the company's policy and plan to push off-label marketing as much as possible even though he and other company executives knew it was illegal under FDA rules.

Peter Chatfield and Phillips & Cohen were brilliant in how they filed the qui tam case against Cephalon. I could not get a lawyer to take the False Claims Act case against Cephalon, and now the full force of the Justice Department was on my side. From that moment in 2006, it became clear that the government was going to win the case.

One of the ways I received more in the settlement was the greater leverage Peter created by filing first on behalf of the state's recovery. All the other relators had filed their cases based on the federal recovery, not realizing there was a state recovery as well. When Peter filed for the state recovery in my case, I was first. First to file in any of these cases makes you king of the hill and in control of the percentage of recovery in a relator share agreement. While state recoveries were smaller than federal, this helped us in negotiations with the other relators.

Cephalon was going to settle, the Justice Department assured me. It was a done deal. I was exultant. My risks were going to yield some rewards. After being nearly hopeless, I finally had something concrete to make me feel optimistic. Protesting against off-label marketing, turning informant, wearing a wire—it all had been justified. The settlement against Cephalon would be proof that my actions were valuable to society and that I had done the right thing. But it turned out to be far from a done deal. I thought an announcement about the settlement would be issued within a few days, and I looked forward to a big check landing in my bank account within a week or two.

The weeks stretched into months. I soon realized that my initial exuberance had been misplaced. That flush of anticipation—of getting life-changing money in the very near future—became tempered by the reality that nothing was happening quickly.

Nobody knew how long it would take. The Justice Department lawyers wouldn't or couldn't tell me anything. They kept telling me that I would know the details when they knew the details.

Peter was a rock throughout the process. I leaned on him as a source of not only knowledge but also calm and stability. We didn't know whether there would be a settlement at all or whether it was going to be in the tens of millions or hundreds of millions. We didn't know how much of the settlement would be set aside to be split up among those who filed qui tam lawsuits. We didn't know how that settlement would be divided among the qui tam plaintiffs—the originator, the first to file, and the relators, those of us who filed later.

Peter offered few particulars but kept telling me to keep the faith. He never said so explicitly and never made any predictions, but my confidence in him reassured me that it really was going to happen and I was probably going to end up with several million dollars. I rarely contacted him, but he was patient with my occasional questions and qualms via email and over the phone. He was very busy with lots of cases, but he always acted like he had all the time in the world to talk to me. That's one of many things for which I'll be eternally grateful to him.

It took months, but when the lawyers for Cephalon and the Justice Department finally reached an agreement on the general outline of the settlement and fines, the deal still could not be announced. The lawyers who filed the qui tam lawsuits for the originator and the other relators still had to agree on how that money would be divided among their clients. In all, there were four people in line for a split of the qui tam portion of the settlement. You might think that would be simple, to split up all that money, but it wasn't. Our lawyers scraped and scrapped and could not agree on how much each of us should get or how much the others should get. This delayed the payout by nearly a year.

While waiting for the details to be worked out for the qui tam portion of the settlement, Peter could have popped some champagne, let the other lawyers work out the settlement, and gone off on his merry way to his next multimillion-dollar payday. But he is not that sort of guy. Instead, he stuck with the tedious, contentious negotiations to get everything he could for me.

I was No. 3 in the sequence of people to file qui tam lawsuits against Cephalon, which meant that I would get a smaller share than the two who had filed first, the originator and the first relator. But everybody agreed that I had been important to the case for wearing a wire. The earlier two plaintiffs were not informants.

In contrast, I had helped make the case, from the first time I called the number Sue had given me for the federal investigators to wearing a wire and gathering the incriminating information from other Cephalon employees. The government lawyers recognized this and wanted my work to be rewarded. I'll be forever grateful that they supported Peter in arguing that I should receive a larger than usual portion of the settlement for a relator who was third in line. They said I was the ideal person—someone who had lost everything by stepping forward to wear a wire—to collect damages under the qui tam provisions. I was the sort of person who should be rewarded the most under the qui tam guidelines.

At one point during those additional months of negotiations over the settlement, Peter had a quiet word with me. "Bruce," he said, "you're about to get an awful lot of money in one very big chunk. I want to make sure you have thought about how you are going to handle it."

I had plans for investing the money, both initially and long range, and setting some aside for myself and my family. I started to think about what I wanted my new life to look like. Many of my roots in Ohio, including my homes and my job, were long gone. Maybe a new start in a new state would be good for me. I had always loved Key West, Florida: one road in and one road out, the last stop in the US.

I explained all this to Peter, who did another one of the things for which I will be eternally grateful: because there was a settlement in principal in place, he was able to get a loan for me of $65,000, with the law firm vouching for it to be repaid in full. When the settlement came through, it would be the first dollars paid out. He didn't have to do that.

I didn't have to sell anything to uproot my residence either. And while $65,000 was a large sum from what I'd seen in the past four years, it wasn't enough for the little island of my dreams. Instead, I settled on Melbourne Beach, a tiny (1.3 square miles, population just over 3,000) aging beach community perched on a barrier island in Broward County, about halfway up the Atlantic Coast. There's not a lot to do; most of the tourism information recommends the beaches, the modest downtown, the pier, and the parks. It is not a rich town. There are a lot of retirees, but most of them are trying to make a limited amount of money last for a while. Just like me when I moved there.

My daughter Michelle came with me, and we rented a small, partly furnished ranch house for $1,200 a month. We arrived in a rickety old SUV with 328,000 miles on it and a couple of seats held mostly together by duct tape. People shouted at us when we stopped at traffic lights, warning about the doors being ajar. They thought they were being helpful, but they weren't telling us anything we didn't know. We said thanks and drove on. We had packed up a big white cooler, four or five feet long, with food and drinks for the trip so we didn't have to spend any money for anything other than gas on the way down. We hauled that cooler into the house, and for the next year it served as our coffee table and our dining table. (Like I said, the place was only partly furnished.)

We'd perch on chairs in the living room or just sit on the carpet and put our plates on the cooler. Other than that, we each had a couple of bags with our clothes. That was it. We got bicycles and rode our bikes around town partly to save money and partly because we were afraid the Suburban would die anytime we took it out.

We made a lot of bicycle trips back and forth to the municipal library, which became sort of a home away from home for us, our public living room. We'd sit and read, we'd attend some of the lectures and programs, and we'd take home bags full of books and DVDs. Our neighbors, most of them retired couples or widows, didn't know what to make of us. Here was this guy, obviously too young to be retired but apparently not working. A few neighbors approached us, carefully, for a little small talk. "I'm just resting here, enjoying the weather," I told them. "Just like you."

No doubt some neighbors sniffed at that—here's this big guy, obviously hiding out, and he wants us to believe this young blonde is his "daughter." I heard some of the whispers. In one version, I was a hit man who had testified against the Five Families in New York. I was in the witness protection program. Nobody was fooled, I was told.

It was my new home for now, though. We didn't share much information with the people in Melbourne Beach, but we didn't share much with the people back home in Ohio, either. I didn't want everybody to know my business, especially when the case was concluding. We could be targets. I was worried about my security. Maybe someone connected to Cephalon would try to take revenge or teach a whistleblower a lesson. Maybe someone would kidnap me or a family member and demand a portion of the settlement. Maybe someone would think I already had the money and would try to rob me. It was mildly reassuring to be so far away from home, in a strange place where we were not known. It would be harder for anyone to find us. But if someone wanted to find us, I knew they could.

We stayed in Melbourne Beach for a year, or I did. Michelle left a few weeks from the end, when she returned to Ohio to take a job. Every day I would wake up thinking, "OK, is this the day? Is this the day I hear from Peter that the money is coming through?

Is this the day I hear from the bank that it has landed in my account?"

Lying low, we spent most of the year in Melbourne Beach, and it was largely uneventful. Boring, even. Life was on hold. We went for walks. We rode our bikes. We went to the library and took out books and read them. We rented movies that we watched together.

Finally, after all the months of bartering among the people who were in line for some of the qui tam money, Marilyn May, the US attorney, threatened to pull the whole qui tam settlement unless the originator and relators agreed to be fair and give reasonable portions to the people who had contributed the most to the government's case, including a Cephalon pain care sales rep who also came into the case as a relator after providing the government with some good inside information on Actiq off-label sales. Unless I got my fair share for taking the risks, doing the work, and making the case, nobody was going to get anything. That ultimatum brought everybody back to the table, ready to make a deal.

Twenty

The Settlement

*T*he settlement was finally announced on September 29, 2008 (see news release in the appendix), almost five years after I contacted the FDA and two years after Cephalon agreed to settle (see the government press release in the appendix). Under the settlement, Cephalon agreed to pay $425 million in fines to the government. The portion of the settlement designated for the originator and relators under the qui tam lawsuits turned out to be $57 million. "Transfer of funds will be soon!" I exalted on page 99 of the fifth volume of my journal.

Under the qui tam agreement, I grossed $17 million as my portion of the settlement—one of the largest settlement awards ever for a relator. I hadn't become a whistleblower to get a payday, so getting anything was a bonus, a small compensation for losing my job and career. Forty percent of my reward went to Peter Chatfield and his law firm as their contingency fee. I was fine with that. It was what we had agreed on. I never would have been involved in the qui tam case and wouldn't have gotten a dime if they had not agreed to take me on and done so much for me. After taxes, I ended up with $6 million.

Throughout the process of the investigation, the lawsuit, and the settlement negotiations, I had learned that nothing happened quickly and that I couldn't really count on anything until it actually happened. So it was with getting the money. I didn't expect to see my bank account explode on September 30, the day after the settlement was announced; the money had to be transferred from Cephalon to the government to my lawyers and then to me. You can imagine what it was like for me, in my little worn rental house in Melbourne, Florida. As much as I was eager to get the money, I was perhaps even more looking forward to having the case over. I used up pages of my journal in calculating how I would immediately use some of the money to pay my bills. I would pay back my mom and Rex and give my kids each a chunk to help them out and start to make up for what they had been through. I would pay off my loans and credit card balances. I doodled around with figures. How much would I be able to afford for a house? I estimated how much I'd spend to buy each of my kids a new car.

The days of waiting turned into a week, then another week. On Friday October 10, I noted in my journal, "No money transferred again. Maybe next week." On Thursday, October 16, going on three weeks after the settlement had been announced, I was told the money was being transferred to my lawyers but it would still take a few days. From my journal: "Tuesday 10/21/08 Money did not get transferred today, but tomorrow it will be in my bank account."

"Wednesday 10/22/08 WOW!"

My friend and former Cephalon colleague John was one of the first people I called when the money landed. He was still employed by Cephalon and approaching retirement. We talked many times on phone calls when I was in Florida. John, quite naturally, always wanted to know whatever I could tell him about the case. Now, with the money actually in hand, I asked John whether I could do anything for him. I was happy to share my sudden fortune with him. It had been his case, too. The phone went silent for a bit, and then John said no, he didn't need or want any of my money. He wanted to lie low and get his pension.

"Hey, man, you love cars. How about I get you a car?" I insisted. There were a few more moments of silence on the phone line, and then John replied, "Well, Frank Baldino drives a black Mercedes SL 550."

I was surprised and pleased. "Done," I said. "I'm getting you that car."

"Hey, Bruce," he said. "You're gonna need a new car, too, and now you can afford one. What are you going to buy?"

I told him I hadn't thought about it. He said, "Maybe we could have matching cars." It seemed like a good idea. Twin cars.

After all, I told him, we were both twins—just from different sets of twins.

I went to the local Mercedes dealership in Melbourne and ordered two matching Mercedes SL 550 cars for a cool $125,000 each. I had one of them delivered to John at his home in Maryland. The other was delivered to the driveway of that little house I was renting in Melbourne. The new car brought my neighbors out of their homes and onto the sidewalk in front of my rental house. "We knew it," one of them told me. "You ratted on the mob, didn't you? And this car is part of your payoff, right?" I just grinned at the neighbor. No need to ruin good neighborhood gossip, true or not. They'd be talking for years about the mobster who used to live on the block.

Incidentally, I drove my Mercedes long and hard and traded it in after a few years. John's Mercedes is still all shiny and has maybe 1,000 miles on it.

The money was nice, but it was anticlimactic at best. I learned a lot about myself. My real wealth was the way my family had become so close.

John called me at one point and said, "You know, Cephalon is laughing at getting away at a cost of only $425 million."

At first I didn't understand what he was talking about. He explained, "Cephalon was ready to pay $900 million. They ended up paying less than half of that, so they regard the fine as a good result. They're happy."

Moreover, John told me, he had heard from people still at Cephalon that the company had no intention of stopping its off-label marketing.

That stunned me. "You're kidding," I sputtered.

Nope, John said. He wasn't kidding. Doing business illegally and then paying a big fine for it was just a normal cost of doing business for Cephalon. The company was going to call it the "Switch Campaign," switching the names of the off-label drugs and switching patients onto the renamed drugs.

Twenty One

The Switch Campaign

*A*fter we settled with Cephalon on a False Claims case for $425 million, the company had plans to continue its off-label marketing even though it had agreed in the case settlement to stop. Actiq was replaced by Fentora, which Cephalon's pain care reps were marketing off-label the same way they marketed Actiq. Provigil was replaced by Nuvigil. The company told doctors who had been prescribing Actiq and Provigil to simply begin writing prescriptions for Fentora and Nuvigil.

I told Peter that Cephalon had basically renamed Actiq but it was still fentanyl and the company was still selling it off-label. He told me that I was still covered by my informant agreement with the government and I had to pass this new information along to Marilyn, the US attorney who had prosecuted the case against Cephalon and reached a settlement. "If nothing comes of it, so be it," he told me, "but you have to tell the government."

So Peter set up a meeting, and he and I returned to Philadelphia to talk to Marilyn. I told her what the company was planning, and she was incredulous. She had always seemed so composed, cool as a cucumber. Now she was upset. The company was agreeing to stop the off-label marketing at the same time that it was laying plans to continue off-label marketing. Fentora, the "new" drug replacing Actiq, was actually stronger and more addictive than Actiq. Cephalon was going to keep marketing it for "breakthrough pain" and for migraines but was going to put a new emphasis on Fentora for back pain, too. I told Marilyn how Cephalon thought the fine had been a bargain for off-label marketing and had been willing to pay much more. "They're laughing at us," I told her.

She slammed her hand down on the conference table and said, "We'll see about that!"

But a second False Claims Act case was not a slam dunk. It was risky, Peter explained to me, for the government to go right back to court. They had just won a big case against this company. If the government lawyers wanted more, they should have gotten it in that first case. This could be deemed harassment. It took the government a couple of weeks to decide what to do, and then Peter called me. "Are you ready to go ahead with another case against Cephalon?" he asked. He said the government thought the danger of more addiction cases and overdoses was worth the risk of filing a second case so soon.

I said no. I had been through enough, and so had my family. Becoming a whistleblower had taken over my life. It had changed me. All I wanted now was a normal life, to return to the way things had been, to be my old self. I didn't yet realize that would never happen. No, thanks, I said. Peter said OK, and I thought that would be the end of it. But he called again a few weeks later. The government thought the settlement could be even bigger in this second case, he said, and I was being promised 15 percent of the settlement as the originator—the first whistleblower. That could be tens of millions.

"Count me in," I said. In September 2008 the second case against Cephalon—and then against Teva, the company that bought Cephalon for $6.9 billion—was filed under the False Claims Act, this one for marketing Fentora off-label. It took years, again, to reach a settlement, and it turned out to be for much less than originally anticipated. In those years, the company moved more fentanyl to more patients, resulting in untold more addictions and overdoses and deaths. Why? We all know why. It's simple. Greed.

I can't help but wonder what more could have been done to stop not just Cephalon and its off-label marketing and the spread of fentanyl but also the entire opioid crisis. As sales reps, corporate executives, doctors, pharmaceutical manufacturing executives, government investigators and prosecutors, public policy makers and members of Congress, how could we have done more to slow the tidal wave of opioid use?

In the wake of tragedy and loss of life, the False Claims cases are cold comfort to the American people affected by the opioid crisis.

Epilogue

*I*t was several months before I moved back home to Dublin, Ohio. From Melbourne, I first moved to my favorite vacation haunt, Key West. I moved to a nice hotel and then into a very nice condo. It was a welcome change to be in more upscale surroundings after the relatively spartan rental home in Melbourne.

It seems like most people who come into some money, like lottery winners, swear that the money won't change their lives. In contrast, I desperately wanted the money to change my life. That isn't what happened. I did buy the Mercedes cars for John and me, and I did repay my bills and give the kids something. But there was no spending spree. I didn't feel like celebrating much, especially with friends who kept inviting me to go out for drinks. I am among the most social animals on earth, but for some reason, in the weeks after I got the money, I mostly stayed home. I didn't feel like going out to restaurants or bars. Maybe there was some sort of psychological letdown from the case finally being over.

Eventually, I started seeing people again and resumed working out. I was able to afford healthier meals and began to feel better. I bought a big house on a golf course in Dublin, even though I don't play golf. I probably—no, definitely—did not need a house that big, but it seemed like a bargain and probably was, since the real estate market was in the tank in 2008–2009. It was a good investment. My only real extravagance was a blowout Christmas party that I threw in Dublin for a few dozen friends who had stuck by me through the dark years. It was a formal bash at a nice hall where men wore tuxedos and ladies wore long gowns and the sit-down dinner featured some of the best food I'd ever eaten. The entertainment was a Motown band, and everybody danced their asses off.

My family still talks about my years as an informant and what that time did to me and to all of us. We all have whistleblowing stories to tell and laugh about. One of my favorites came from all the phone calls I got related to the case when it wasn't yet clear that Cephalon was going to lose and that I would be a winner. I took those calls 24-7. If one of the investigators was calling, or one of the Justice Department attorneys, one of my qui tam lawyers, or a former Cephalon colleague who wanted to talk about what was happening at the company, I wanted to take those calls. There were innumerable conversations and gatherings—restaurant dinners, cocktail chats, barbecues, parties, and more—where I pulled my phone out, answered the call, and then walked off so that no one else could hear me. It became my signature move, and the kids began joking among themselves, whenever we got together, about how long it would take for me to get a call and walk away. My son, Eric, had the best line. "What if," he asked his sisters, "Dad was not really getting calls? What if he was just acting like he was getting all these important top-secret calls? What if Dad isn't really an informant? What if Dad is just crazy?" We all loved that and still joke about it. A few months after the case settled, Michelle called me and said, "Hey, Dad, remember that big diving trip we were all going to take together someday, before this all started? Let's do it now." And so we did it. We finally got our big family diving trip.

Today I am closer than ever with my kids. I don't know anyone else who has a better relationship with their grown kids. I have great relationships with many of the other people who stuck by me, including my brother, Rex, and my friends Dave and Becky, who basically saved my life by giving me work flipping burgers at their festival. I still show up at the food stand once in a while to do a shift, cutting onions, taking orders, preparing hot dogs. "Look at this," Dave sometimes crows to customers. "This is such a classy place that we have a millionaire working the booth."

But I wasn't yet finished with Cephalon and off-label marketing investigations and qui tam lawsuits. Despite that huge settlement that the company had to pay, Cephalon continued its off-label marketing. The government had Cephalon dead to rights again but didn't pursue the case with the same vigor. Marilyn left her position as US attorney, new investigators were assigned by the FDA, and it seemed like a smaller, less important case.

Another factor, perhaps, was that the criminal charges disappeared when Frank Baldino died in 2010 and prosecutors did not follow up with charges against any other Cephalon executives. Frank's obituary in the *New York Times* mentioned Provigil in the first paragraph—not as a narcolepsy treatment, which was its original intent, but rather for its widespread but off-label use to increase alertness.

A year later, Cephalon was still one of the most successful biopharmaceutical companies in the world, with more than $2.8 billion in sales. With the death of Frank Baldino, its guiding force and inspiration, the company seemed rudderless, but it was still a major player in the pharmaceutical world. The company was acquired by the Israeli drug conglomerate Teva, the largest generic drug company in the world, for $6.8 billion in 2011. Eight years later, Teva paid an $85 million fine to the State of Oklahoma in the first round of lawsuits brought by states against the major producers of opioids, including Purdue Pharma and Johnson & Johnson.

The second Justice Department case—and my second qui tam lawsuit—loomed, but it had become a smaller case, with diminished importance. Peter and his firm decided not to represent me the second time around. I easily found another firm to represent me, but that case didn't settle until 2017. "And it is over!"

I wrote in my journal, on page 117 of volume eight. "After 14 years you are done with Cephalon!!"

In 2010, I was invited to be part of a group called SWAT (Successful Whistleblowers Advocating Against Taxpayer Fraud). The author Kitty Kelley interviewed us when we got together in Washington, DC, and described us as "men and women whose exploits have commandeered front-page headlines, been heralded on *60 Minutes* and *Dateline*, and, not incidentally, helped enrich the U.S. Treasury by over $16 billion."

Kitty's article, published on her website, emphasized that only 1 percent of whistleblowers receive "life-changing" money. She also noted that even whistleblowers who come away with substantial qui tam settlements are "are not happy-go-lucky moguls, reveling in the wealth they earned by taking principled stands against fraud and abuse and corruption." The article tells how I lost my job for refusing to follow my company's orders to promote drugs for "unapproved," off-label purposes.

"Most of us gave up years of our lives in litigation and lost all we had, to tell the truth," the story quotes me as saying. The story reports that despite my multimillion-dollar award, I still felt "ostracized from society."

"All of us do," I told Kitty. "We're looked on with disfavor and disgust by people who think we're crazy or, even worse, greedy. There's a stigma for telling the truth in a go-along, get-along world."

I'm pleased that people are interested in my story as a whistleblower. I filmed a segment of the CBS series *Whistleblower* that effectively went back through my life, starting with my folks and growing up in Dublin, Ohio, through my pharmaceutical career and then my whistleblowing, the legal battles, and, finally, the aftermath for me personally. I was asked whether I had tried off-label marketing myself, and of course I said that, yes, I had. However, I added, "I didn't do very well at all with selling off-label. Because my heart just wasn't in it. I didn't think it was right."

The filming gave me a new appreciation for what I had done and the impact it had—and the impact it didn't have. It also gave me new insights into the turmoil it caused my family and the heavy price we all paid. The CBS crew filmed me at their studios in New York, at my home and elsewhere in and around Dublin, and in Nevada. We spent two days in and around the Westin Lake in Las Vegas, the resort where I wore the wire for the OCI investigators during the Cephalon national sales conference in early 2003.

It was a hoot being back there. The crew even brought a drone and sent it up overhead to film me re-creating the walk away from the hotel when the agents told me to get out of the hotel while they badged the two Cephalon trainers and tried, unsuccessfully, to flip them to become informants, too. The timing of that walk away from the hotel was such that CBS captured me literally walking into the sunset.

Some of the filming got emotional. I broke down several times when I was being interviewed one-on-one and being asked to relive some of the toughest moments in those long years of wandering in the wilderness, wondering whether Cephalon would be prosecuted. I broke down when the producers had me reciting the litany of losses I had suffered as a result of becoming a whistleblower: my wife, my family, my job, my house, my cars. I had no partner, no money, no job—and at times, it seemed, not much reason to live. I also broke down more than once when the producers handed me portions of my diary to read on camera. Looking back, I know now that it was that positive attitude from a grateful heart that got me through those years.

At one point I was standing in my kitchen in Dublin with my daughters, and the cameras rolled as we talked about what it was like back when I started being a whistleblower. I hadn't realized how difficult it had been for them, how much it affected their everyday lives, and how much they worried about both what was going to happen to me and what was going to happen to them. Before long, the tears were rolling down all three of our faces. I suppose it made for great TV, but for me it was a moment of great personal insight. I have always felt bad for the huge disruption I imposed on their lives, but after hearing it from them, firsthand, I felt even worse.

My lawyer, Peter, was a very good on-air interview. Judge Alex Ferrer, the host, led Peter through the theory, the evidence, what is needed in a qui tam case, the obstacles and problems in this particular case, and how the government overcame them—in large part through the evidence that I brought to the table as a whistleblower. "In light of the opioid crisis that we all know about, would it be fair to say that Bruce was the canary in the coal mine?" Alex asked my lawyer.

"I think, with hindsight about what has happened, he absolutely was, yes. We had never seen anything like that. And you can see what happened. It took off from there," Peter responded.

The CBS producers were ecstatic with it because they had been puzzling over how to present the complexities of the case, and especially the qui tam and other legal aspects, in a way that a general TV audience could understand and appreciate. Peter took care of all that for them. He was so smooth, so concise, so accessible, so understandable. He made this whole sprawling mess of Cephalon and off-label sales so easy to understand, so logical.

In the big scheme of things, I have to wonder whether the government investigators, FDA, and Justice Department could or should have done more to crack down on opioids back then, when I was an informant. It's a fair question, given that today the country is suffering tens of thousands of deaths per year from opioid overdoses and related overdoses of heroin and other drugs, along with untold suicides related to opioid abuse. It's been the big health crisis in America in recent years.

Opioids were not a big deal in America in the early 2000s. Most Americans had not heard of fentanyl, or how it was perhaps the most addictive and deadly dangerous of all the opioids, until Prince died of an overdose of fentanyl at his Paisley Park mansion in Minneapolis in 2016. But we can see the lethal legacy dating back to Actiq, which was supposed to be used only for breakthrough cancer pain.

Prince did not have cancer or cancer pain, nor did the vast majority of the people who took Actiq, supplied via Cephalon.

Nor do the vast majority of the people who have taken and abused fentanyl and other opioids. I'm always going to wonder about how and whether Cephalon—and I and my sales rep colleagues at the company—can be blamed for contributing to the rise of opioids and the subsequent opioid crisis. If Cephalon had not pushed Actiq off-label, would fentanyl have become as popular as it is today? Would it have remained merely as a niche drug for breakthrough cancer pain? Would it not have become such a widespread pain? Would it not have become such a popular supplement to heroin among abusers and addicts looking to get the highest high? Would opioids in general and fentanyl in particular have killed as many people? Would fentanyl have become a common product of illegal labs, often in China? Would it have come to account for more than half of the nation's opioid-related deaths in recent years? If we had not introduced so many people to this newer, stronger form of opioid, would other forms of opioid drugs be as common today? Would the death tolls be as high? Would the nation as a whole be less reliant on opioids? Cephalon didn't cause the opioid crisis, but its aggressive off-label marketing of fentanyl may have opened the door and rolled out the red carpet for this highly dangerous drug.

There are other things I wonder about. What if the federal government had come down harder on Cephalon and other drug companies that were just getting into the business of promoting opioids for wider use among the general public? What if the Department of Justice had contemplated criminal charges not only against Frank Baldino but also against some of the other

Cephalon executives? They, too, were culpable in pushing sales reps to promote Actiq off-label and in spreading its use from a relatively small group of cancer patients with breakthrough pain to the much wider universe of anybody who had migraine pain or other types of more common, everyday pain.

Were the pharmaceutical executives manufacturing and mass marketing opioids any less guilty of damage to society than, say, heroin or meth dealers? Or terrorists? Some would argue that drug abuse, especially of opioids, has had a more harmful impact on more Americans and American families than all the terrorists and acts of terrorism put together in recent years. Did our government agencies, charged with protecting us, miss the opportunity, back in the early 2000s, to stop the opioid epidemic?

And what about the physicians who prescribed opioids? What about the doctors back in 2003 who put too much trust in Cephalon pharmaceutical reps and prescribed this little-known, highly dangerous drug to patients who didn't need that kind of risky medication? Don't those doctors bear some of the responsibility for abdicating or ignoring the best interests of their patients? To do no harm? Do pharmacies and drug stores bear some of the responsibility, too? Pharmacists are supposed to be experts in medication: what drugs do, how they work, and, especially, how they can be abused. Shouldn't more pharmacists, instead of simply being good soldiers following orders, have raised the alarm when they saw patients abusing opioids and becoming addicted?

I can't answer those questions. I don't know whether anyone can really answer them. Sometimes people come up and want to congratulate me or thank me or talk to me when they find out I was involved in blowing the whistle on fentanyl. One of the sound technicians on the CBS crew told me he had raised his hand for this job because he had a nephew die of a fentanyl overdose.

I have to wonder, though, did I really make a difference in exposing opioids? Even inadvertently? I can never know whether my whistleblowing kept the opioid crisis from being even worse today. But I take consolation in knowing that I tried to do something.

So we come back to the questions that everybody asks me: If you had to do it all over again, would you? Knowing what you know now, having lost so much, having been through so much, would you still become a whistleblower? First, I'd like to make the point that the money from the settlement, while substantial, while nice, while a great compensation, was certainly not a good reason to become a whistleblower. Remember that I didn't know the money was a possibility when I first put on a wire. I had never heard of qui tam. I was just trying to do the right thing. Another important point: the money from the Department of Justice settlement was compensation for what I had lost. I had been pretty well off when I became a whistleblower.

But, again, the money was not why I became a whistleblower. I was trying to do the right thing. That's still what is most important to me. I have to wonder: If I had not stepped up, would anyone have? How many innocent patients might have been injured or killed by off-label drugs that were prescribed to them because a sales rep misled a trusting physician? How many more drugs would Cephalon have abused through off-label sales? How many other drug companies would have followed Cephalon's lead? After all, off-label sales, despite some collateral damage to patients, were a proven way to increase profits, thanks to Cephalon's example.

Would I do it again? Would I become a government informant? Would I wear a wire? In the first years after becoming a whistleblower, it wasn't easy to answer those questions.

Now, the answer is a little easier: Yes, those years of poverty and misery and self-doubt were difficult. Thinking about the worst times of the bad years—even at the lowest point, when I was most despairing of what had happened to me, most worried about what was going to happen to me, and most uncertain about whether I would ever have a fulfilling, productive life again—I can say with certainty that I would do it again. It was the right thing to do.

That's especially true, looking back, because of what has happened with the opioid crisis. It is gratifying to be called "the canary in the coal mine" for the opioid crisis, but it is disappointing to know that my whistleblowing was not more effective and didn't do more to stop the opioid epidemic. But I hope my whistleblowing did at least a little to alert government officials and pharmaceutical industry executives about the dangers of fentanyl and other opioids and to warn them about the dangers of off-label marketing by drug company sales reps. For those possibilities alone, it was all worth this wild ride.

What did I get out of being a whistleblower? I became a better person, I think. That's the great reward, not the money. It's the glow inside that comes from fighting for a cause bigger than yourself—and winning. Being a whistleblower was self-development for me. I learned how tough I really was.

I had to ask myself sometimes: Can you cut it with all these very smart people—relators, lawyers, agents, and even judges? You are in the big arena. A lot of that didn't hit home until I was invited to the US Senate. I traveled to DC with Peter to appear before a Senate committee and to be recognized for my contributions to society as a whistleblower.

I feel empowered by what I have accomplished. It's a great feeling knowing that you did make a difference. You are an individual who made a difference. I think we all can. For the right reasons—a greater cause—you can achieve anything. Never give up. You have to be committed. Money doesn't work. That's a misconception. You have to be committed.

I have also been enriched by friendships, including in Florida, both at Melbourne Beach and Key West. After the settlement came through, I moved my residency to Key West from Melbourne Beach. Melbourne Beach was more of a surfing town, and Key West was more of a fishing town. I had to satisfy my Florida residency before I could move back to Ohio, but after the settlement came through, I could do something I love—blue water sportfishing: wahoo, mahi mahi, tuna, sailfish, and blue marlin.

It was a beautiful sport for enjoying my newfound days in the sun. But that wasn't what was really important in Florida. It was the friends I made in both Key West and Melbourne Beach, especially the woman I met while looking for a rental house in Key West. She not only became a great friend and confidante but also introduced me to her family and friends and helped me create a new social circle. What a plus in life to realize what is really important. It's not money or fame but real love, where people have your back and it is not about your wallet. I will be forever indebted to those friends, just like I will always be indebted to Becky and Dave for giving me a job flipping burgers at $10 an hour. I wish everyone in life could find those kinds of special people and moments that so enrich life.

Would I do it all again, so as to open up the new parts of my life—such rewards beyond money?

Hell yes.

A Few Words for Potential Whistleblowers

*W*hen I started this journey, I expected certain outcomes that never existed—the outcomes were way better than I could have imagined. A big reason for that is my lawyer. Without Peter Chatfield and his firm, Phillips & Cohen, none of these outcomes would have come to pass. He and his colleagues were all helpful through the entire process, often above and beyond the call of duty.

Why is it important for people to know about whistleblowing? First, it's against human nature. Most people would not—and do not—become whistleblowers. They don't want to rock the boat or take the risk of reprisals and retaliation. We go along to get along.

I was just one person who stepped up. But maybe my story will encourage one other person to step up someday, somewhere:

maybe in the pharmaceutical industry, some other corporation, government, law enforcement, or neighborhood nonprofit. I recently heard about a volunteer treasurer for a local Little League team who had been stealing money from the kids' dues for years—until a parent figured out what was going on and blew the whistle with the other parents.

There's not one single path for whistleblowing. Every example of wrongdoing happening in secret is different. Every thief or fraudster is different—and every whistleblower is different. But if you find yourself in the position of possibly blowing the whistle, don't automatically reject it. Don't automatically turn away from wrongdoing just because turning away is safer or less of a hassle. Don't help sweep things under the rug. Don't help the bad people keep doing bad things. Shine a light. Like the investigative journalists say, sunlight is the best disinfectant.

If you do find yourself considering whether to blow the whistle, especially when doing it like I did—from inside a company, a government agency, or another established institution—there are how-to guidebooks that advise on keeping yourself safe and being effective. But I'll give you the four things that I'd advise any potential whistleblower:

1. **Get the right lawyers early in the process**—if possible, before you blow the whistle. If you think it may lead to a False Claims Act action, seek out a good qui tam lawyer.
2. **Understand the evidence.** Just because someone is doing something wrong doesn't mean that person can

be stopped or punished. You need evidence related to the fraud. You need to know what proof is needed, and whether you can produce it, in order to build a whistleblower case.

3. **Think hard about getting that evidence** and gathering it most effectively without exposing yourself.

4. **Know, perhaps with the help of your lawyer, what you are going to do with the evidence.** Whom are you going to give it to? What will they do with it? I turned my informant evidence over to the federal agents handling me. I turned more evidence over to my lawyers for the qui tam case. But you might also consider ombudspeople or internal investigators or journalists. Keep copies of everything you pass along, and write a journal with names, dates, and places.

As a whistleblower in general, and as a relator on a qui tam suit in particular, you need to be aware of the dangers to you personally, both financially and emotionally. Some people don't fall apart. They soldier on, holding it all together. I fell apart, and you now know after reading about my difficult years.

I speak often to business, professional, and civic groups about whistleblowing and what it means, especially to the whistleblower. I tell my story, professional and personal and as a whistleblower, to individuals and groups about ethics and morals in the workplace and how to step up as an individual. I don't want to tell anybody what to do or give any sweeping lectures to people about being ethical or moral or doing the right thing. I just tell my story, and if it helps you or your team or your company, great.

If your endeavor is centered around a common cause for good and not wrapped up in egos—either the whistleblower's or the lawyers'—you can accomplish anything. I really believe that if work is done for the right reasons and rooted in good for society, then all is possible. It becomes bigger than an individual and any egos. It's not about you.

And it's not about the money. No one should become a whistleblower thinking that it will turn into a big payday through a qui tam lawsuit. I was fortunate. Most whistleblowers are not that lucky. I could just as easily still be painting houses and flipping burgers today, broke and depressed. I have never talked to another whistleblower who went into it thinking about a qui tam settlement and then came away with a meaningful award. The most successful whistleblowers are the ones whose efforts resulted in some change for the public good and who came away from the experience satisfied with themselves and what they did. No successful whistleblower I ever met went into it for the money.

Instead of being greedy themselves, they were fighting greed and the greedy practices that put people's lives at risk. Fewer than one out of 10 whistleblowers looking for a life-changing qui tam settlement get one. It took me 14 years to get my settlements. You don't make money in the kind of extended time frame we typically see in whistleblowing and qui tam lawsuits.

You have to commit to something bigger than money, and you need the heart and internal fortitude to survive the journey.

Sometimes when I speak in public or lead workshops, I am asked how people can step out of their routines, out of their safe lanes, and do something for the greater good. That's the biggest obstacle. I was a good worker bee, following orders, staying in my lane. And I was richly rewarded for it. Whistleblowing was my rebellion in life, after a life of trying to be who I was supposed to be and who others wanted me to be—parents, teachers, bosses, family, colleagues.

Giving up the "good boy" part of my life was liberating. I was still intent on being a nice person—gentle, considerate, kind, empathetic. But I became a risk taker, an activist with everything on the line. And I changed as a person as that side of me grew. I came to realize that I am a natural optimist. To me the glass isn't just half full; it's brimming, it's overflowing. I have learned to see the best in every situation and the best in every person. But I have also become more realistic. It was difficult for me to recognize and accept what was happening with off-label marketing at Cephalon and even harder to recognize and accept that it was happening solely out of the company's greed.

But once I realized the scope of the problem, I couldn't stand by and let it keep happening. My natural optimism helped me believe I could make a difference: if I stepped up, things would get better. Without that faith that I could make a real difference, I might not have taken the risk of whistleblowing. I knew wearing a wire was the start of something that could lead to a rough time in my life, but I did it anyway because I had a core belief that things were always going to work out for me in the end. That belief, like many of my beliefs, was sorely tested during my whistleblowing, and I saw how naive I was.

The lowest point was when I imagined my kids actually saying out loud what I had been thinking: "Dad, what have you done to us? Give it up. We've lost everything. Stop. Let it go. Start over." But none of them ever said that. Instead, it was always, "Keep going, Dad. It's going to be OK. We love you and support you, and we're proud of you." It was tempting to walk away sometimes and stop being an informant, but I didn't feel like I could do that. I couldn't walk away. I had to see it through. I just felt, somehow, that things would work out.

Things are great now with the kids, who are all on their own and doing well. I can do the nice things for them I couldn't do during those trying years. I get along well with my ex-wife, Beth—still the love of my life, though I know we'll never get back together—and she sometimes refers to the person I once was, the old Bruce, the Bruce back then. But my kids know me and refer to me as the person I am now. I'm very happy with that, with the new Bruce. My whistleblowing experiences changed me from bashful and naturally embarrassed—a result of my upbringing—to an outgoing guy, eager for new people and new experiences. Whistleblowing brought out the carney side of me, literally. Working the food stand was pure work, and the physical exhaustion was soul cleansing somehow.

I still don't know where I am going in life, what I am going to do, what is next. I'm in my sixties but don't feel or think like an older person. Adventures lie ahead. More opportunities—and more risks. I am open to everything and anything.

I like and am proud of who I have become.

If you become a whistleblower, be prepared to get to know yourself as never before. I developed as an individual, as a human being, in ways that I never would have. I realized how strong I was internally, how I called on my internal constitution and fortitude and belief in myself to carry me through. You learn a lot about yourself when you lose everything and have to rebuild your life. As JFK said, "Those who dare to fail miserably can achieve greatly."

News Release: September 29, 2008
"Cephalon Pays $425 Million to Settle Whistleblower Off-Label Marketing Case"

WASHINGTON, DC—The government's investigation, initiated by a whistleblower lawsuit brought by Phillips & Cohen, into Cephalon Inc.'s illegal marketing practices that culminated in today's $425 million settlement and guilty plea by the pharmaceutical company began in January 2003 with a Cephalon sales representative in Ohio.

The sales representative, Bruce Boise, refused to follow company-ordered sales strategies to convince doctors to prescribe Cephalon's Actiq, Gabitril and Provigil drugs for unapproved (off-label) uses because he was worried the sales practices were illegal and the "off-label" uses were dangerous for patients.

Boise was so concerned about Cephalon's off-label marketing that he contacted the Food and Drug Administration (FDA) to inform them of what the company was doing and then agreed to wear a wire to a company sales conference to help the government gather evidence.

The decision to report Cephalon to the FDA cost Boise his job and future employment in the pharmaceutical industry. But his information helped end Cephalon's illegal marketing practices that put patients at risk and led to today's settlement.

Cephalon Inc. (Nasdaq: CEPH), a pharmaceutical company based in Frazer, Pennsylvania, will pay the federal government and numerous states a total of $375 million to settle four "qui tam" (whistleblower) lawsuits alleging Medicare and Medicaid fraud involving the sales and marketing of Actiq, Gabitril and Provigil between 2001 and 2006. At the same time, Cephalon has agreed to plead guilty to a criminal charge involving off-label marketing of drugs and will pay a $50 million fine.

"What makes this case unique is that it's the first time, in the absence of substantial kickbacks, that the federal government has used the False Claims Act to go after a pharmaceutical company for marketing drugs for off-label indications for which there were no credible published scientific research supporting these drugs' safety or effectiveness," said Peter W. Chatfield, a Washington, DC, attorney whose firm, Phillips & Cohen LLP, represents Boise. "Not only were these uses marketed by Cephalon not approved by the FDA, there was absolutely no literature published in any medical compendia that supported them."

The FDA approves drugs for specific uses, which are noted in the drugs' labeling. Doctors may prescribe those drugs for other "off-label" therapeutic uses, but the law prohibits drug companies from promoting drugs for uses beyond those found to be safe and effective by the FDA.

While Medicare, Medicaid and other federally funded healthcare programs often will pay for off-label use of drugs supported by credible medical research and prescribed based on the medical judgment of physicians, Cephalon's marketing efforts pushed well beyond those constraints.

Cephalon's off-label sales strategies were very effective. The government's investigation found that more than 80 percent of the sales of Provigil, Gabitril and Actiq were for off-label uses.

The FDA approved the use of Provigil to help keep awake patients with certain disorders, such as sleep apnea or shift-work sleep disorder. To boost sales, Cephalon marketed Provigil for off-label uses including fatigue associated with mental illnesses, such as schizophrenia, and children with attention deficit hyperactivity disorder, according to Boise's lawsuit.

Gabitril was approved for the treatment of partial seizures in epileptic patients. Yet Cephalon was pushing doctors to prescribe it for anxiety and insomnia, Boise's lawsuit said.

The most dangerous Cephalon drug when used for "off-label" uses is Actiq, an opioid that is approved only to treat cancer patients when their usual pain medication doesn't control "breakthrough" episodes of extreme pain. The potential side effects of Actiq include nausea, dizziness and respiratory depression, which can be life-threatening.

Boise's lawsuit says that Cephalon decided to increase Actiq's sales by marketing it for general pain treatment to internists and general practitioners—doctors who usually aren't as familiar as oncologists are with the potential dangers associated with using a prescription narcotic such as Actiq.

Boise was the first to report Cephalon's off-label marketing practices to the federal government and played a key role in the investigation. Only after he was fired and found it impossible to secure new employment in the industry because he had been blackballed did he seek counsel to file a lawsuit under the False Claims Act. The whistleblower law allows private citizens to sue companies defrauding the government and receive a reward. But by the time he hired a lawyer to represent him, nearly two years had passed since he first contacted the FDA.

In the interim, two other whistleblowers filed qui tam lawsuits making similar allegations nine months after Boise had provided extensive information to the FDA and reported Cephalon to the FDA. After he learned about the False Claims Act, Boise contacted Phillips & Cohen, which filed his qui tam lawsuit in federal district court in Philadelphia, Pennsylvania, in September 2004 on behalf of the federal government and a dozen states with similar false claims statutes. A fourth whistleblower filed a qui tam lawsuit one week later.

Today's settlement covers all four whistleblower lawsuits. The whistleblowers will receive a reward totaling $46 million for their information and the work on the case they did with their attorneys on the federal case and roughly an additional $11 million for the state cases.

"Bruce Boise sacrificed a lot to protect patients across this country," attorney Chatfield said. "But he found Cephalon's practices to be so outrageous and dangerous that he has no regrets about going to the FDA despite suffering more personal hardship than any whistleblower I have ever represented."

Chatfield praised the work of Assistant U.S. Attorney Marilyn S. May of the Eastern District of Pennsylvania and William C. Gambrell Jr. of South Carolina's Medicaid Fraud Control Unit, who coordinated the efforts of the states to evaluate losses to the Medicaid program.

Phillips & Cohen is the largest and most successful law firm that specializes exclusively in representing whistleblowers nationwide in qui tam and tax fraud cases.

Case citation: U.S. *et. al ex rel.* Boise *v.* Cephalon Inc., C.A. No. 04-4401 (Eastern District of Pennsylvania).

CBS News Press Release, June 28, 2019
"Lollipop Made With Powerful Opioid Fentanyl Was Illegally Marketed, Ex-Pharma Rep Says"

Bruce Boise said "every day was different" even "exciting" to him as a pharmaceutical salesman at Cephalon. But that all changed in 2000 when he says he was ordered by his boss to promote drugs "off-label" to doctors—meaning for purposes that were not approved by the Food and Drug Administration—in order to boost sales.

"It's not legal for a pharmaceutical company to promote off-label," said Dr. Christopher Gharibo, a NYU pain specialist.

"I didn't do very well at all with selling off-label, because my heart just wasn't in it. I didn't think it was right," said Boise, who shared his story with host Alex Ferrer in the "Whistleblower" season finale, "Opioid Lollipops: The Case Against Cephalon." So, Boise took action and contacted investigators at the FDA. They wanted proof the company was breaking the law.

"A couple of agents . . . sat down and talked to me about what the company was doing and asked me to bring material to show how they were doing it," Boise explained.

In 2003, agents asked Boise if he'd wear a wire at a Cephalon national sales meeting.

"I thought if that's what . . . it took to stop a company from doing what they're doing," he told Ferrer.

Boise was outraged when he heard a sales rep describe how he was promoting Actiq, a medical lollipop made with the extremely powerful opioid fentanyl to general practitioners.

"Fentanyl," Dr. Gharibo explained, "is a very strong opioid. It's about a hundred times stronger than morphine."

Fentanyl is the drug that killed Tom Petty and Prince and, according to Gharibo, "very easy to overdose on."

The FDA had approved Actiq only for cancer patients in acute uncontrolled pain—a very small market. Cephalon, though, pursued a much larger one. "They eventually marketed it," Boise said, "for low back pain and migraine patients."

"You're talking about a Class 2 narcotic," he said. "And you're giving it to a migraine patient . . . So it puts patients at risk." Boise was fired when the company learned he was working with the FDA—and then his fears about promoting Actiq for off-label use were realized: Robin Geist-Wick, a migraine sufferer who took Actiq to dull her headaches, tragically, became addicted.

"It hooked her right away," Robert Wick said. "I wish Robin had never taken that Actiq. I think she'd still be alive."

Peter Chatfield is Boise's whistleblower attorney.

"In light of the opioid crisis that we all know about, would it be fair to say that Bruce was the canary in the coal mine?" Ferrer asked Chatfield.

"I think with hindsight about what has happened, he absolutely was," he replied. "We had never seen anything like that. And you can see what happened—it took off from there."

Boise did not sell Actiq himself, but he heard a Cephalon sales rep give a presentation about how he marketed Actiq to general practitioners at their national sales meeting where he wore a wire for the FDA. He also received specific information about their promoting Actiq for migraines and lower back pain from a colleague who worked directly in Actiq sales.

Boise did receive a financial reward for blowing the whistle; it was a portion of Cephalon's settlement with the government. The court awarded him $17 million. After taxes and legal fees, Boise took home $6.5 million. That was one of the largest rewards in this season's Whistleblower stories.

About the Author

*B*ruce Boise spent more than twenty-four years in the pharmaceutical industry, as a hospital representative, and then as an area manager in the Great Lakes region. From 2003 to 2017, he worked with the United States Justice Department on two separate False Claims Act cases against Cephalon/Teva, a neuro-biotech company. The first case settled for $425 Million USD and was covered in the CBS show Whistleblower, season 2, episode 4 in 2019. Today, Bruce's advocacy efforts include mentoring other whistleblowers and educating people on the importance of whistleblowing for consumer safety. He's an Ohio native.